Chicago History:
The Stranger Side

FACT, FICTION, FOLKLORE, AND "FANTOMS"
OF THE WINDY CITY

RAYMOND JOHNSON

Illustrations by Kimberly MacAulay

Schiffer Publishing Ltd

4880 Lower Valley Road • Atglen, PA 19310

Dedication

To history yet to be unearthed.

Other Schiffer Books by the Author:
Chicago's Haunt Detective
ISBN: 978-0-7643-3718-5   **$16.99**

Designed by RoS
Type set in 2RebelsDeux/NewBskvll BT

ISBN: 978-0-7643-4509-8
Printed in The United States of America

Published by Schiffer Publishing, Ltd.
4880 Lower Valley Road
Atglen, PA 19310
Phone: (610) 593-1777; Fax: (610) 593-2002
E-mail: Info@schifferbooks.com

For the largest selection of fine reference books on this and related subjects, please visit our website at
www.schifferbooks.com.
You may also write for a free catalog.

This book may be purchased from the publisher. Please try your bookstore first.

We are always looking for people to write books on new and related subjects. If you have an idea for a book, please contact us at
proposals@schifferbooks.com.

Schiffer Books are available at special discounts for bulk purchases for sales promotions or premiums. Special editions, including personalized covers, corporate imprints, and excerpts can be created in large quantities for special needs. For more information contact the publisher.

Contents

Acknowledgments ...4

Introduction ...6

The Chicago Courthouse and an Elmhurst Haunting ...9

The 1893 World's Columbian Exposition Fire and the Secret at Oakwoods Cemetery ...29

The Devil, The White City, William Green, and The Cook County Sheriff ...47

The Haunted Palace of Lincoln Park ...65

Chicago and the R.M.S. *Titanic* ...75

The Search for Peabody's Tomb and the Masochistic Monks? ...99

Voice of the Grimes Sisters' Killer? ...111

The Tonic Room Witch ...131

Haunted History of a High School Landmark ...141

Conclusion ...153

Bibliography and Suggested Reading ...154

Index ...155

Acknowledgments

"rooted and built up in him, strengthened in the faith as you were taught, and overflowing with thankfulness."

Colossians 2:7

No work of fiction or NON-fiction
can be written without the help of MANY.

Don and Kim MacAulay
Kirsten Tillman and Beth Shields of Paranormal Stars
Rick and Susan Sherman
Matt Maziarek, Mark Betz, and the whole CPR gang
Colleen Carroll, Jim Prewitt, and the ASP gang
Denise Vanaria
Bruce Beveridge
Brian Bergheger, Nancy Wilson, and Lance Tawzer of the Elmhurst
Historical Museum
Thomas Rusnak, Drama Teacher and Theater Manager Extraordinaire
Mark Sujak, Chodl Auditorium Manager, J. Sterling Morton East
High School
Mary Ellen Jenicek, J. Sterling Morton East Archives and Library
Phil Costello and the whole gang at the Cook County Clerk of the
Circuit Court Archives
Chrissie Howorth, Janneke Fowers, and Kathi Wagner of the Mayslake
Peabody Estate/Forest Preserve District of DuPage County
The Hippach Family
Kathleen Herrebout, Mary Kelly Greene, and the whole Kelly Family
Tom Waits and the whole Tonic Room gang
Nefer Khepri Ph.D.
Jack Connors, Frank McMenamin, and Father John McNalis of the
Fire Museum of Greater Chicago
Paul Lutz and Kyle Nauert

A very special thanks to my wife, Laurie, my sons, Kevin and Mikey,
and the rest of my family and friends for seeing mostly the back of my
head during the writing of this book.

Introduction

I have always been a big fan of history and especially a fan of local Chicago and suburban Chicago history. About the only time I didn't like studying the old times was when I was in school. I don't know if it was just me, but it seemed like history was an endless stream of dates, names, and places that had absolutely no relation to my life or what I was planning on doing the coming weekend. Lucky for me I had an amazing memory for that type of thing, but usually the memory lasted only for as long as I needed it to—that was usually right up until I chose the A , B, C, D, (or E if you had a really tough teacher) on the weekly test. Right after I turned my test in, I couldn't tell you if Lincoln was president during the Civil War or the Cold War. Okay, maybe I was not quite that bad, but frequently, in order to really learn something, it had to be relatable and interesting to me. And most times, once I actually did learn something, it could take a while to forget it, if I ever forgot it.

It wasn't until I started researching the genealogy of my family that times past started to come alive for me. Suddenly, I had a second great-grandfather who fought in the Civil War, and all those dates, names, and places began to mean something to me. And so it started.

I have also been interested in topics that are a little off the beaten path—parts of history you don't read about in school: legends, folklore, unsolved mysteries, and hauntings.

Couple all of that with a natural curiosity and need to solve puzzles, and that is probably what led me to a career in criminal investigations... and then you *get* my first book, *Chicago's Haunt Detective*.

As I was continuing my research into the stranger side of Chicago's history, I soon discovered that in addition to the fun and fascinating history of Chicago ghost stories, there were times that history itself could be as entertaining, which brought me to the writing of this book.

Don't get me wrong, I love a good ghost story, and there are plenty in here, but there is also a little strange history that can be just as spirited.

Chicago has enough history to keep an army of writers busy for a number of lifetimes, and the city has done just that. In fact, before the first person reads this book, I should be well on the way to finishing the next (if my readers and publisher will have me). So sit back and enjoy and, if this tome is entertaining enough, maybe some of the names, dates, and places might stick for you as well as they have for me.

The Chicago Courthouse and an Elmhurst Haunting

A number of years ago, I became acquainted with the fascinating history of Elmhurst, Illinois, when I was writing a series of articles that discussed bits of Chicago history that you could find within the city's many suburbs. I was familiar with Elmhurst for a good part of my life because of its close proximity to where I currently live, the fact that the church I attend is located there, and that it was also home to the Elm Roller Skating Rink (demolished in 1989) where I had gone on a first "date" of sorts with my future wife.

There are many links between Elmhurst and the city of Chicago and one of those links is a souvenir of the Great Fire of 1871 and the collector of that souvenir, Seth Wadhams. I became aware of the souvenir when I was attending a church function in what is currently Elmhurst's "Wilder Park," named so because it is part of the estate of resident Thomas Wilder who passed away in 1919. The Elmhurst Park District acquired the estate, including the Wilder Mansion, in 1921, and sold the mansion and one acre of land to the City of Elmhurst for $14,000. The remaining land became Wilder Park.

As I was walking through the park, I noticed something that looked similar to a large cement garden decoration, but on closer inspection I saw a small plaque that had been placed in front of the piece and it read:

Elmhurst Landmark
1870
Urn-Adorned Cook County Court House before Chicago Fire of 1871
Marked by the Elmhurst Bicentennial Commission
Martha Ibbetson Chapter of NSDAR

Being a history buff, it really peaked my curiosity as to why a piece of the Chicago Courthouse would be sitting in the middle of a public park in Elmhurst, but I didn't really look into it much, until about two years before writing this book.

THE TRAGEDIES OF SETH WADHAMS AND FAMILY

Thomas Wilder was not the first resident of the "Wilder Mansion." The original builder of the structure was a man by the name of Seth Wadhams.

In 1868, Seth purchased a treeless farm called "Burnhams Lot" and built a home, calling it "White Birch." At that time, Elmhurst was still known as "Cottage Hill." Seth Wadhams (1812-1888) and his wife, Elizabeth Reed McKinney (1816-1882), were originally from Connecticut. Seth was born in Goshen, Litchfield, Connecticut, on October 29, 1812, to David Wadhams and Pheobe Collins. He was the 13th of 16 children. He and Elizabeth (daughter of a physician) married in Connecticut on June 4, 1849, and had two children of their own: a daughter, Emma, in 1850, and a son, Dana, in 1852. They also adopted a boy named Frederick Eugene Holland, who was born on January 26, 1853, in New York and later became a Chicago physician. They came to the Chicago area sometime after 1853. Seth became a millionaire ice dealer, founding the Wadhams, Willard & Co., in 1859.

Wadhams surrounded his new home with as many species of trees as were able to survive in the climate. He also hired a landscaper, gardener,

Finial Urn from the top of the Chicago Courthouse as it sits today at Wilder Park in Elmhurst, IL.

Landmark Gardens
1870
Very-Adorned
Cook County Court House
before Chicago Fire
of 1871

The Wilder Mansion as it looks today.

and herdsman to care for the property. In fact, it was Wadhams, Jedediah Lathrop, Thomas B. Bryan, and several others who are credited with planting a large number of elm trees along Cottage Hill Road, which inspired the name change to "Elmhurst."

In addition to the home, Wadhams built a greenhouse for his wife, to help her to overcome her grief over the death of her young son, Dana Wadhams, who passed in 1858, at the age of roughly six years. This greenhouse, still in use today, is located to the rear of the Conservatory and is the forerunner of the extensive horticultural activities that are currently taking place in Wilder Park.

Seth's daughter, Emma, was somewhat of a rebellious free spirit and initially followed her father's directives, marrying the son of a prominent Chicagoan named Edward R. Loring on March 15, 1870. She lived in Peoria for a number of years, but later divorced Loring, without her father's knowledge, in order to marry an architect named Walter R. Colton. Her father was furious and told her that she was forbidden to marry Colton, and if she did, she "would never blacken my door again!" On June 10, 1875, she married Colton, walked out, and never returned.

Seth's wife, Elizabeth, died on July 8, 1882, shortly after Emma had left and Wadhams soon found himself alone and, by all accounts, a broken man.

Seth Wadhams seemed to have had a change of heart concerning never wanting to see Emma again and for years searched for her, even enlisting the help of private detectives, but to no avail. Seth Wadhams died in San Diego, California, on February 6, 1888, never to have known the whereabouts of his daughter, or even if she was dead or alive.

Wadhams left a large part of his estate to his adopted son, Frederick, as well as leaving sizeable amounts of money to various charities of Chicago, including $30,000 to the Old People's Home of Chicago, which was located at Indiana Avenue and 39th Street. He left the money with the stipulation that it be used to fund the building of a home for elderly American-born men. He also stipulated that his homestead of "White Birch" be offered for sale at the price of $20,000 to Mrs. Henry (Aurelia Case) King, daughter of Seth's lifelong friend, John R. Case, and wife to Henry W. King, who was owner of one of the largest clothing firms in the country.

In April of 1911, some twenty-three years after the death of Seth Wadhams, a 62-year-old woman stood in the doorway of the Old People's Home. Her name was Emma Wadhams Green. This was indeed the long-lost daughter of Seth Wadhams. It seems that Emma's second husband, Walter R. Colton, had died a few years back and she was now married to a poor man named Green, who was staying with relatives in Michigan. She had no way of supporting herself and was looking to the Home for assistance. They told her that her father had left a good amount of money to the institution and that they could give her a couple of

Photo of Seth Wadhams. circa 1880.
Photograph courtesy of the Elmhurst Historical Museum, Elmhurst, IL.

dollars per week to sustain her. She accepted, but soon after, hired an attorney named John Colburn to look into the matter of her father's estate. Following a legal battle of roughly four years, the courts sided with Emma Green. It seemed that though her father had donated the money to the Old People's Home with the stipulation that it be used to build a home for elderly, American-born men, it had merely been invested for twenty-two years. Her lawyer argued that since the money was not being used for its intended purpose, it should revert back to Mrs. Green. In November of 1915, her appeals finally paid off, and since Frederick Wadhams (her adopted brother), had passed away in 1913, the $30,000 plus interest (currently $86,000) was awarded to Mrs. Emma Wadhams Green, her father's sole living heir.

Following the death of Seth Wadhams in 1888, the property changed hands twice until it was purchased by Thomas Wilder, in 1905, eventually offered to the City, and ultimately the Elmhurst Park District.

In 1923, the Elmhurst Park District Board added a conservatory to the original Wadhams greenhouse. The conservatory was erected by the American Greenhouse Manufacturing Company for a cost of $6,950. In 1926, a second greenhouse was built by the Foley Greenhouse Manufacturing Company for a cost of $2,350. In subsequent years, the Park District added a storage area and a third growing house.

Today, the conservatory, greenhouses, and Wilder Park gardens continue to provide beauty and serve the varied interests of Elmhurst residents.

In 1922, the Elmhurst Library moved into the first floor of the building. In 1936, an eight-month remodeling project was finished, which completely changed the exterior of the building, added pillars and a south wing, and removed partitions on the second floor. A second addition was completed in 1965.

Sometime after the remodeling and additions had taken place, there were reports of a resident "mischievous spirit." Employees of the library reported that books and other artifacts were being moved from one location to another without the help of a living assistant. It never seemed to be a malevolent entity, just more of a nuisance than anything.

In June of 2012, I started conducting haunted tours of the historic areas in Elmhurst, along with Kirsten Tillman and Beth Shields, who are paranormal investigators (www.paranormalstars.com). In the course of giving tours, we had the opportunity to speak to several people who have had ghostly experiences at The Wilder Mansion. In one such account, a young woman mentioned that when she was a child, she remembered going into the Mansion (Elmhurst Library at the time) and that as she

Seth Wadham's home as it looked when he occupied it.
Photograph courtesy of the Elmhurst Historical Museum, Elmhurst, IL.

walked through the front door, there was a stairway off to the left that led to the second floor. She heard a female voice calling her name from the second floor and she started to walk up the stairs to investigate. As she was ascending the stairs, headed toward the voice, she noticed a slight fog coming down the staircase from the second floor.

In another account, a woman was told by her grandmother that when she was in the library doing research on the Holocaust of World War II, a woman wearing a vintage-style dress came up to her and asked her what she was researching. When her grandmother glanced back at her book to give her the title, the woman had just disappeared.

Some individuals believe that the Mansion is haunted by the spirit of Seth Wadhams, who had never planned on his homestead becoming a library or being renovated without his approval. Some believe that he may be angry because the daughter he had written out of his will came back, after the death of both of her parents, to receive a huge chunk of inheritance that she was never meant to receive. Still others believe that the spirit could easily have been the tormented spirit of Elizabeth Wadhams, who had lost her son, Dana, at the tender age of six, and who died before ever knowing the whereabouts or condition of her only daughter, Emma.

If you believe that energies or spirits can be somehow attached to a structure or location after a traumatic event, then there might be a reason why the area could retain the remnants of an energy from long ago.

THE SPECTER OF THE CHICAGO CITY COURTHOUSE AND JAIL

Seth Wadhams was also a bit of a souvenir collector. On October 8, 1871, the fledgling City of Chicago was engulfed in flames. When it was over, 17,500 buildings were destroyed. One of those buildings was the Chicago/Cook County Courthouse, whose bell tolled the alarm that alerted the city to the fire. Seth Wadhams had sent a wagon into the city and retrieved two of the cement urn-like capstones from the top of the courthouse, bringing them back to his property. One still remains near the southwest corner of the Wilder estate. In fact, that capstone is one of approximately a half dozen of the capstones that were salvaged from the rubble by various collectors.

The "Spirit of the Jail" was a well-known ghost story in the city before the Great Conflagration of 1871. One of the best documented accounts of the ghost was in the December 11, 1867 issue of the *Chicago Daily Tribune*. Deputy Sheriff Edward Langley was on his watch at the county jail, around the end of October, when he heard a great moaning unlike any he had ever heard from a human being. It resonated through the prison at about 11PM, long after the prisoners had been locked down and had nearly settled to sleep. It was quiet after the sound, but he had without a doubt heard the moan, although the only sound he could hear now was the occasional scampering of a rat. In fact, he had heard several prisoners conversing before the unearthly noise, but it was obvious that they were intently listening as well. He made rounds through the several wards, asking prisoners if they had heard a noise, and they all confirmed the reality of the moan, and many were still visibly shaken from the experience. After a short time, the moaning returned, and this time it was much louder than before! Every time he looked for the origin of the moaning, it seemed to change location. This noise that he described as "most unearthly and awful" continued at irregular intervals for the next hour, before it finally ceased. He did not report this initially to other authorities for fear of being thought a lunatic.

Two days later, he was with Deputy Sheriff Merrill in the same office when the noise started up again! It sounded as though it could be the sound of a person in horrible agony and seemed to be coming from a vault at the end of the hallway that was being used as a water closet (bathroom). Upon closer inspection of the water closet, they opened the bolt on the door and could hear the sound coming from beneath their feet! It then seemed to change direction again and came from the eastern limits of the jail. They quickly returned to the office and were forced to listen to the noises for the first half of the night!

About a week later, Deputy Sheriff Tuttle and Simpson were on watch when, at 10 p.m., they heard a repetition of the same sound. This time Tuttle seized a light and traced the screaming to cell 18. As he stood outside the door with his light, waiting to catch one of the prisoners who was probably making the noise, he was extremely startled by the noise coming directly below his feet! The shock stayed with him for many days to come.

Stories of the phantom of the jail started spreading rapidly among the prisoners, and one night, an African-American prisoner by the name of William Jones saw the apparition of a man hanging by his neck from a strap that was attached to the grating, leading to the ventilator, from the ceiling. Jones stated that he was so terrified that he fainted from the experience, and for the next several weeks, various Deputy Sheriffs had taken similar reports of a hanging apparition.

Talk amongst the prisoners and jailers seemed to point to the likely culprits of William Corbett and Patrick Fleming, who were executed by hanging on December 15, 1865, in the eastern most section of the jail, for the murder of Patrick Maloney on November 20, 1864.

The End of Patrick Maloney

The beginning of the end of Patrick Maloney seemed to start some months before his murder. Maloney lived in the area of Sand Ridge (now the Austin neighborhood of Chicago) near where John Pierson had built the Six Mile House, a two-story tavern, in 1842. The Six Mile House would now be at the northwest corner of about N. Pine Avenue and Lake Street. Maloney belonged to an Irish family that was in a virtual war with another Irish family of which John Williams was a member. Nobody can remember what the feud was about, but everyone seemed to have been of the opinion that it was somewhat trivial. Neighbors had to intervene quite often to keep one from killing the other and each family was known to have taken shots at the other family's dogs at a time when the owner was conveniently closest to the dog! The 19th Mayor of Chicago, John Blake Rice (1809-1874), lived in the same area and was heard predicting that one would probably eventually kill the other, if both didn't die in the process.

It seemed that neither family had any money, although John Williams had saved some from selling prairie grass. (I'm not sure how much money could be made from selling prairie grass or how much the going rate was, but okay...) Unfortunately, the most important use Williams could come up with for the extra change in his pocket was to hire some poor saps to assassinate Maloney.

According to reports, sometime in early to mid-November 1864, Fleming, Corbett, and another Irishman by the name of John Kennedy were at a drinking establishment when approached by a stranger (presumably Williams), who had contracted with them to assassinate Maloney. They were supposed to have gotten about sixteen dollars each, but according to their testimony, had received no money at all.

On November 20, 1864, the trio met with an acquaintance, James Finan, who supposedly had no idea of their intentions to kill Maloney. They met at Phillip Brennan's Saloon at 117 Canal Street for drinks and told Finan that they needed to know where Patrick Maloney lived because they had to visit a sick aunt of his. They hired a "hack" (1860's horse and buggy version of a taxi) and Brennan supplied a driver named William Gubbins. They instructed Gubbins to take them to the vicinity of the Six Mile House and they stopped at a number of drinking establishments on the way, as well as bringing a full bottle of whiskey with them for good measure.

When the whiskey ran out, they decided that it was time to get down to business. Finan, Kennedy, Corbett, and Fleming exited the hack and told the driver to extinguish his lights. The driver did not want to get in trouble with the authorities for having extinguished lights, so Gubbins simply turned the vehicle around, so that anyone in the direction of where they were heading would not see the lights. Finan accompanied Kennedy, Corbett, and Fleming to show them where Maloney lived, still believing the "sick aunt" story he was told. The hack was stopped about three blocks from the house of Maloney and Finan got close enough to the house to point it out to Kennedy, Fleming, and Corbett. He then returned to the hack.

They went to the front door and Kennedy positioned Corbett at the side of the door. Kennedy had a navy revolver, in case Corbett couldn't do the job. Kennedy instructed Corbett to shoot Maloney as soon as he could get a good shot. Maloney was woken from his sound sleep by Fleming's loud knocking on the door. Maloney asked who was at the door and one of the men answered, "A friend!" Maloney refused to answer the door and they attempted to force it open. As the door started to give way, Corbett fired his revolver once at Maloney and supposedly had missed.

This inflamed Fleming and Kennedy, who cursed Corbett for his lousy marksmanship. Maloney, now realizing that he was fighting for his life, struggled that much harder, but he was outnumbered. Honora heard the commotion and joined her husband at the door. Corbett fired once more through the door and this time the resistance was eased, as Maloney fell down screaming his wife's name, "Honora! Honora!" Honora saw the shadows of the three assassins fleeing from the house and her husband lying in a pool of blood. Her five young children were crying, and as she cradled her youngest child close, her husband, Patrick, died in her lap within ten minutes. She spent the entire night holding her children and her dead husband. All three men returned to the hack and spent the rest of the night celebrating their short-lived victory.

Months went by, and while John Williams, James Maloney, and Michael McDermott, neighbors and enemies of the murdered man, were brought in for questioning, nothing solid came of it. The break came when officers learned that a hack owned by Phillip Brennan had been hired to take a group of men to the area of Sand Ridge on the night that the murder took place. Police found out that the regular driver of the hack was sick that night and that a man named William Gubbins was hired for the job. It took five months to locate Gubbins and question him about that night, but he talked very freely and gave accurate descriptions of the men who he believed perpetrated the crime. He mentioned to police that he would have come forward sooner and on his own, but he was afraid for his life, in case one of the murderers would somehow escape and come after his family.

The second break in the case came when, on April 23rd, Fleming and Corbett were arrested for an unrelated assault (actually attempted murder) of policeman Peter Kendelin of the Second Precinct. Corbett had managed to stab Officer Kendelin multiple times, but Kendelin still managed to arrest him. Fleming fired multiple gunshots at Kendelin but none of the shots hit their mark! (Some nerve after complaining about Corbett's marksmanship during the Maloney murder.) Fleming was arrested the next morning and the two were sentenced to fourteen years in the State Penitentiary in Joliet. Unfortunately for them, police officers don't take kindly to those who try to kill one of their own, and because of this, pay special attention to those who do. Captain Kennedy of the Second Precinct and Sergeant Hickey of the First Precinct recognized them from the descriptions given them by hack driver, Gubbins, and arrested them for the murder of Patrick Maloney, as they were being led to their cells to await transfer to Joliet. Gubbins positively identified them as two of the persons involved in the murder of Patrick Maloney.

Once Corbett and Fleming were secured, it was only a matter of a week's time before an informant mentioned to Captain Kennedy that James Finan had told a mutual friend at a saloon on Polk Street about his involvement with the Maloney incident. Finan was arrested and immediately turned state's evidence, providing the final name, John Kennedy, who was apprehended the same day.

The evidence against Corbett and Fleming was overwhelming. Damning testimony of Mrs. Honora Maloney, James Finan, and William Gubbins soon sealed their fate. The jury returned a guilty verdict in a little over two hours of deliberations. On Saturday, November 26th, in the Superior Court Room of the County Courthouse, Judge Gary was prepared to pass sentence on Corbett and Fleming. Kennedy had somehow managed to get a separate trial in Waukegan.

The judge ordered Corbett and Fleming to stand up and approach the railing beside the clerk's desk. Corbett was physically shaking and placed a trembling hand upon the railing. Fleming fixed a combative stare upon Judge Gary. Gary continued, "Have you anything to say, either of you, why the sentence of the law should not now be passed on you?" Fleming defiantly answered, "Yes I have!" and looked straight at Judge Gary. Judge Gary simply responded with a pause and then, "Well?" Fleming started right in:

> You are to pass sentence of death on me, for the murder of a man I never seen and never knew. I never laid a hand on him. I never conspired against him. I might have rode out in a carriage, but I never knew him before or afterwards; and it is just on the night he was killed. I never knew the man was going to be killed. Thank God, I never raised my hand against him. I am not afraid to meet death in any form. I have one remark to make in reference to Mr. Reed [prosecuting attorney]. He made the remark that I would kill a man for money. All the money you ever seen, or ever will see, I would not take a life for it. Yourself are in the habit of taking more bribes than me, and it is well known in this city you have, and I am right!

Judge Gary then asked Corbett if he had any remarks and Corbett responded, "I have nothing to say." Judge Gary continued:

> Patrick Fleming and William Corbett: You have been indicted for murder, tried and found guilty in accordance with all the forms of law. No one who listened to your trial, can doubt of the justness of the verdict. It now, only remains for the Court to pronounce the sentence of the law. In doing this, I shall not comment upon the circumstances of your offence, or reproach or upbraid you

as to its enormity. By what inherited disposition, defect or wickedness of early education, real or fancied injustice or injury, moral warp or political bias, you may have been led to the commission of this horrible crime, has not appeared. If the history of your lies were divulged, perhaps the feelings of men toward you might be softened. But society cannot endure that you should live. It must, by every means in its power, protect itself against your kind. Nor shall I address to you any exhortations. I will only remind you that there is no earthly hope for you. It will be utterly in vain for you to expect executive clemency. Few in this community would even sign a petition to the governor in your behalf. The law requires that the day of your execution shall be fixed not less than fifteen, or more than twenty five, days from this time. Usage has settled that capital punishment shall be inflicted upon a Friday. The sentence of the Court, therefore, is, that you, Patrick Fleming and William Corbett, be taken from the bar of this Court to the prison of Cook County, there to remain until the fifteenth day of December, in the year of our Lord 1865, and on that day, between the hours of ten o'clock in the forenoon and four o'clock in the afternoon, within the walls of said prison, or within a yard, or enclosure, adjoining such prison, that you be hung by the neck until you are dead.

Both men turned around immediately and quickly took their seats again. Fleming made eye contact with most in the room in a somewhat disdainful manner, almost searching for some look of sympathy or doubt and it was quickly apparent that everyone in the courtroom was satisfied that a just sentence was handed down. Corbett, on the other hand, looked as though he was actually remorseful about his involvement and could look at no one. He merely looked straight down at the floor. Deputy Sheriffs Merrill and Langley (who were witnesses to the moaning ghost of the jail in 1867), along with Deputy Sheriff Stone, shackled the prisoners and escorted them to where they would spend the final two weeks of their lives, cells 1 and 2 on the very east side of the jail in the basement of the courthouse.

For the next roughly two weeks, Corbett and Fleming were in almost constant care of their spiritual advisors. Both men were Catholic and were almost daily attended to by the Rev. Dr. McMullen of St. Mary's University, Father Burke of the Church of St. Columbkille, and Father Murphy of St. James. They were also attended to by the Sisters of Mercy and the Sisters of Charity who actually handcrafted the burial shrouds of the two condemned men. They received Holy Communion every other day and spent most of their time reading the Bible and other books on religion.

The night before the executions, preparations of the gallows were made. Corbett and Fleming were moved from the eastern most cells 1 and 2 to the western most area into cells 14 and 15, so as to minimize their knowledge of the preparations at hand. However, the hammering noises involved could be heard resonating throughout the entire courthouse. The same gallows had been used for four previous executions, although only the last one was held in the same location as Corbett's and Fleming's.

The first Chicago execution was that of John Stone, who was hanged, in 1840, for the murder of a neighbor, Mrs. Lucretia Thomson. Both lived about nine miles northwest of the city. The hanging took place in public on the prairie about half-way between the termination of State Street and the Cottage Grove Cattle Yards. (Today, that would be at 22nd Street. and Prairie Avenue or just on the north side of the McCormick Place West Building.) The public was invited in mass to attend the execution in order to provide protection for the officials, in case there was an attempt to rescue the prisoner. There was no attempt.

The second execution was that of William Jackson on the 19th of June in 1857. Jackson was convicted of murdering a person by the name of Roman Morris on the road near Libertyville in Lake County. He was taken from the courthouse along Lake Street to the West division, Madison Street to the Bull's Head, and from there to the place of execution between Polk and Taylor Streets, where there were more than 10,000 spectators. The next execution took place on the 20th of April, in 1858, when Albert Staub was hanged for the shooting of a farmer named Lanermann over an argument over the Prussian Government.

About three months later, on the 1st of July in 1858, Michael McNamee murdered his wife, Jane McNamee. Both McNamees indulged in alcohol and while Mrs. McNamee was prone to acting in ways to excite her husband's jealousy, Mr. McNamee was an extremely distrustful and passionate husband, which didn't make a great combination. On the 6th of May 1859, McNamee was hanged in the county courthouse in the same location that Fleming and Corbett were about to meet their fate.

The scaffold had been the same used since 1840 and, in the courthouse, they positioned the large wooden beam at the landing at the top of the staircase on the eastern most part of the courthouse. At the top of the stairs were the debtors' room on one side and the women's room on the other. The beam would be rested on the casements of the door leading to these two rooms at a height of about seven feet, with two wooden supports nailed to it and resting on the ground. Directly beneath this were trap doors that opened downward from the middle and created an opening 3'7" wide by 5'3" long, which was ample room for two men to be hanged at the same time. Two holes were cut in the beam above in which the two nooses would be fed through and knotted at the top of the beam. The drop would occur when a spliced cord, attached to a pair of iron levers, was pulled with about a half-pound of force (a typical pistol trigger pull is about 2-3 pounds of force). Once the trap was opened, the doomed men were to fall until their heads were about 18 inches below where they were standing on the trap. The object was to administer enough drop force with a properly tied hangman's noose that would generate the force required to dislocate the prisoner's spinal cord from his brain, which was intended to cause instantaneous death.

Unfortunately, this drop method was the older way of executing people by hanging and prone to mishaps. An improperly dropped person or tied knot could cause the condemned individual to die a slower death by strangulation, rather than a clean separation of their spinal column. The newer method, which hadn't been implemented yet in Cook County, consisted of a 300-pound iron weight attached to the hangman's noose, which was dropped from a considerable height, resulting in the victim being yanked upward rather than being dropped, which was much more efficient. Regrettably for McNamee (the most recent execution of six years ago), things did not go as planned. At the drop, the rope around his neck broke and McNamee fell about fifteen feet to the basement below. They quickly recovered the poor fellow, reset the gallows, and attempted a second drop, which didn't break his neck, and he strangled for about fifteen minutes before he was pronounced dead.

On the day of their execution, both Fleming and Corbett seemed to have an air of confidence about them. Fleming's was more because of his disdain for the justice system and Corbett's more from a spiritual peace that he had made with his maker, with assistance from the many priests and sisters who had visited with the pair over the prior weeks. Corbett had made a full confession to State's Attorney Reed regarding the shooting of Maloney and blamed his demise on "bad whiskey and bad company." Corbett also said that while Fleming did not fire the fatal shot, he had admitted to Corbett that prior to this he had murdered three other men, but had gotten away with it. They were given the opportunity to inspect the burial shrouds that were handmade for them and while Corbett seemed disinterested, Fleming seemed to pay close attention to the white muslin shroud that had a large black cross on the front covering a larger white cross. There were two smaller black crosses above the arms of the larger cross and then two white crosses below the arms.

As the courthouse bell tolled noon, further immediate preparations were being made, as the scheduled time of execution was about two hours away. Corbett was given a cigar to smoke, while Fleming a clay pipe. Both men seemed extremely calm, given the circumstances, so much so that one of the guards had made a comment that one of the priests must have slipped the men some marijuana in place of tobacco. Both men were wearing crucifixes and rosaries around their necks and intently listening to the prayers being recited by the clergy in their rooms. Dr. Murphy was formerly a chaplain in the 58th Illinois Regiment and had met Corbett on an earlier occasion when Corbett was a deck hand on a Mississippi riverboat, which seemed to give Corbett some comfort. The men had already been lead through the prison by deputies, saying their last goodbyes to other inmates they had met, and they also made peace with Finan who had turned them in, as well as the third in the deadly trio, Kennedy, who was locked up pending his separate trial in Lake County.

As the two o'clock hour struck, deputies started escorting those out who were not given special permission by the sheriff to attend. Fleming and Corbett spent their last thirty minutes in constant prayer.

At 2:30 p.m., Sheriff Nelson entered the cell and shook hands with them. Corbett had nothing to say, but Fleming, while shaking hands with Nelson said, "Good bye, good bye, Mr. Sheriff." They were led down the hallway toward the east end of the corridor by Sheriff Nelson, with Father Roles next to him. Fleming followed close behind between Father McMullan and McGowan. Corbett was between Father Sullivan and Murphy. Off to the sides and behind were Deputy Sheriffs C. Folz, Gustave Fisher, T.M. Bradley, William Wayman, Harry Pease, and Charles Henney. About thirty persons, including members of the press, were present as they approached the stairway to the floor above where the gallows had been prepared. They passed under the large wooden beam and took their seats on two armchairs on which hung the white shrouds and caps that they were to be executed in. Corbett was dressed in a grey suit and Fleming had on a black and white velvet vest, black pants, and boots. Both Fleming and Corbett carried a crucifix in their hands and, at times, would be fixated on it and kissing it multiple times. Both men were quite pale and Fleming seemed to be the less nervous of the two. Father Roles, in a loud tone, uttered the latin phrase, "Attentis!" A silence fell over the group as Sheriff Nelson stepped forward to read the death warrant. With the formalities completed, the sheriff asked the two men if they had any words to share. Corbett replied, "I have nothing to say, but I give you all my blessing and I hope we will meet in a better world." Fleming spoke up, "I am very thankful for your kindness and I hope you will be rewarded, and I hope God will bless you; I forgive every one that ever injured me, and I hope if I have injured any one, they will forgive me." Both men bade a final farewell to the deputies and clergy and Corbett had actually kissed a couple of them. The time had come and, at 2:43 p.m., they were helped to their feet, over the wooden trap through which they would exit this world. Their hands and feet were bound and they could no longer hold the crucifixes to their mouths, so Father McMullen held them to their lips. The Deputies covered them in their white shrouds and tied the drawstrings along their collar. Deputy Fisher adjusted the noose on Corbett's neck while Bradley adjusted Fleming's noose at 2:46 p.m. They both kissed the crucifix for the last time and the white caps were placed over their heads. While you could no longer see the men under the shrouds and caps, you could hear their loud prayers mingling with those of the clergy. At 2:49 p.m., the trap was opened and the bodies of both men fell through in an instant. The ropes grew taught with a "thud" and the elasticity of the rope actually caused the bodies to bounce slightly. For about three minutes there were involuntary muscle spasms and, at 2:53 p.m., all motion, save for a slow swinging to and fro, had ceased.

A step ladder was brought over and Drs. R.L. Rea and J.W. Freer examined the bodies, pronouncing them dead. White pine or poplar coffins that had been painted black were brought over to just below the feet of the executed. At 3:08 p.m., Deputy Bradley cut Fleming's rope and his body lowered into the casket, Corbett's was treated similarly. The rosaries and crucifixes were removed from their necks, although the scapulary that Corbett was wearing was allowed to remain according to his last wishes. The white caps were removed and their faces were revealed to be slightly discolored with bulging eyes and swollen protruding tongues indicative of the physical signs of death by hanging. The bodies stayed overnight at the jail and, in the morning, were turned over to the County Undertaker, who temporarily placed them in the old cemetery vault. Father McMullen arranged to have the bodies permanently buried at Calvary Cemetery at the Church's expense to keep the bodies from falling prey to the "Resurrectionists" (body snatchers).

JOHN KENNEDY'S FATE

(No...not *that* John Kennedy!)

John Kennedy's attorney had managed to receive a change of venue for his trial because he convinced the judge that a guilty verdict and execution of Fleming and Corbett could bias potential jurors in Kennedy's case. He was granted the change of venue and his trial took place in the Lake County courtroom in the northern suburb of Waukegan. Unfortunately, the change of venue was about the only advantage that Kennedy had gotten, because the testimony and facts of the case were identical to that of Fleming's and Corbett's and an identical finding of guilt was the end result.

As Kennedy was led into the courtroom for sentencing, he stopped and looked at the ceiling above the doorway and saw the small aperture in the ceiling through which the noose would be hung. All of the workings of the gallows took place behind the scenes, where above the ceiling and over a beam is a 273-pound iron weight, suspended and attached to the free end of the noose, thereby jerking the individual off of his feet and dislocating his neck.

Judge Williams, with Kennedy's wife listening intently, read the following in open court:

> The sentence of the Court is that you be taken by the Sheriff of this county on Friday, the second day of March next, from the jail of this county, and that you be hung by the neck till you are dead, and may God have mercy on your soul.

Kennedy was immediately taken into custody and his wife broke down on the front steps of the courthouse crying, "My John to be hung! My husband to be hung and I am to go back to my children alone!" She started to rave, stomp, and shout as though half insane, and then started down the road to the depot. State's Attorney Reed and others collected money for her at the depot and presented it to her with a show of sympathy to her, but none for her husband.

After a slight delay, Kennedy was brought into the same courtroom, on the 27th of July 1866, to be executed. He stood below that opening in the ceiling, but this time the noose was waiting for him. He was very pale and so nervous that he could barely stand. The clergy attending him whispered words of encouragement in his ear and helped him to

Stereograph card of the Chicago City Courthouse after the fire of 1871; the finials are visible on the top of the roof. *Library of Congress, Prints & Photographs Division, [reproduction number, LC-USZ62-57059].*

his feet. By 2:30 p.m., Kennedy, the last of the trio responsible for the murder-for-hire of Patrick Maloney, was dead.

Could the hauntings of the Wilder Estate (formerly Seth Wadham's White Birch) be due to the irritation and resentment of Seth Wadhams, the overwhelming sadness of his wife, Elizabeth, or even the possible remnants of past executions somehow recorded into the very structure of a souvenir from a haunted courthouse? It could very well be from all three or none of the three, but I found it very interesting that paranormal investigators Kirsten Tillman and Beth Shields managed to record an EVP (electronic voice phenomenon) near the Great Fire relic of what sounds like a male voice saying, "I wish they'd let me smoke some."

The 1893 World's Columbian Exposition Fire and the Secret at Oakwoods Cemetery

Ever since I can remember, I have had a fascination with the 1893 Chicago World's Columbian Exposition. I am not sure exactly why I am so fascinated by the Exposition or why it holds special significance. If I believed in reincarnation, I would probably say that in a former life I had something to do with, or at least attended, the great fair. I know many people who are so obsessed with the history of the *Titanic* that many of them believe that they may have been passengers on the ill-fated ship in a former life and some even take it to the point of identifying with particular passengers. I can't say that I identify with anyone in particular who planned or participated in the fair, but if I was alive at the time, you can bet that I would have. I even have plans to start a non-profit group in the future—Friends of the White City—dedicated to educating today's students on the historic significance of the fair to the city of Chicago and the world, as well as raising money to try to help preserve what is left of the fair in the way of buildings, artifacts, and documents.

The formal beginnings of a U.S. fair commemorating the 400th anniversary of Christopher Columbus's voyage to the Americas started with the introduction of a bill entitled, "A Bill to Provide for a Permanent Exposition of the Three Americas at the National Capital in Honor of the Four Hundredth Anniversary of the Discovery of America." (Whew! Say that in one breath!) Once the bill was introduced in Congress, it immediately grabbed the attention of some major U.S. cities whose administration believed that Washington, D.C. should not be the only city considered as a host city. The major contenders were considered to be St. Louis, Washington, D.C., New York, and Chicago, with St. Louis being dropped from consideration first. Washington had large tracts of available land, but almost no private resources. New York had wealth and size, but the only area large enough would have been Central Park and that drew quick opposition by New York residents. Chicago had large tracts of land bordered by Lake Michigan, sizable private resources and, with twenty-four different railroads having terminals in Chicago, it could boast one of the biggest and most efficient transportation systems for both humans and freight. Congress passed a joint resolution on February 25, 1890, which was approved by President William Harrison on April 28th. Two organizations were formed to oversee the planning and execution of the fair. The World's Columbian Commission, which consisted of two commissioners from each state and territory appointed by President Harrison and the stockholders of the Chicago corporation formed to promote the city as host.

What amazes me most is the fact that the planners, engineers, architects, laborers, and service people had only two years to go from idea to the magnificent reality that we have come to know as "The White City." What was equally amazing to me was the fact that the city of Chicago had virtually burned to the ground only twenty years earlier, and from these ashes, would rise the greatest World's Fair the world had ever known. The fair occupied over 600 acres in and around Jackson Park with 14 "Great Buildings" including the Manufacturers and Liberal Arts Building that was over 1/3 of a mile long and took up 1,327,669 square feet or roughly 23 football fields! There were an estimated 65,000 exhibits by individuals, businesses, 47 states and territories, over 50 foreign nations, and 39 colonies within the great buildings, as well as over 200 additional buildings, 61 acres of newly created lagoons and canals, a food service capable of feeding 30,000 people per hour, a private security and fire service (Columbian Guard) of over 2,000, the debut of George Ferris's Wheel, which was over 264 feet high and capable of carrying over 1,400 passengers on 36 separate cars that were the size of buses, and over 27.5

million visitors from opening day of May 1, 1893 to closing on October 30, 1893.

I could go on and on about the grandeur of the fair and plan to do just that in some of my future endeavors, but I wanted to concentrate on one particular day of the Columbian Exposition that peaked my interest.

Each day of the expo had its high points and low points, and July 10, 1893, was a particularly low point.

The police and fire services have a mutual respect for one another and work very closely together. I formed many friendships with firemen over the years when I was a criminal investigator and that is probably why I was first taken by this story. On the afternoon of Monday, July 10, 1893, four Chicago firemen, eight firemen hired by the Columbian Exposition, and three civilians lost their lives in a fiery inferno that was the cold storage building. It was the greatest loss of life in the Chicago Fire Department, until the Chicago Stockyards fire of December 22, 1910, which claimed the lives of Chief Fire Marshal James Horan and 21 firefighters.

The Cold Storage Building, which was owned and operated by the Hercules Iron Works Company out of Aurora, Illinois, was located just east of Stony Island Avenue and south of 64th Street. It would have existed roughly where the Jackson Park field house exists today. Fire Marshall Murphy had stated before the disaster that the Fire Department was going to have a problem with the building. He believed it to be a virtual "fire trap." (I always believed that this should have been the beginnings of the phrase "Murphy's Law," which states that "whatever can go wrong, will go wrong." I understand that the accepted start of the phrase didn't occur until much later when a Captain Edward A. Murphy, who was an engineer working on Air Force Project MX981, cursed a technician who had incorrectly wired a transducer and said, "If there is any way to do it wrong, he'll find it." The project manager kept a list of "laws" and wrote this one down as "Murphy's Law" in 1949. I believe that Chicago should take back "Murphy's Law" as one of its own, but I digress.) The building was not technically a "Fair" building, but was more of a concession that was utilized for cold storage by the exhibitors, as well as providing ice for exhibitors and patrons alike. It was 6 stories high, with an ice skating rink on the top floor and three 120-ton "Hercules" icemaking machines on the ground floor that visitors could see in operation. The building was 150' x 255' and had an observation tower on each corner and a large smokestack running up the middle of the building that was 191 feet tall. A wooden enclosure surrounded the smoke stack and gradually narrowed as it reached the top. The first 50 feet above the roof was very plain looking, but as it narrowed, it included ornate columns that supported platforms and ended a mere 10 feet from the stack, while supporting a wooden cupola that was flush with the top of the stack. That much wood dangerously close to a 191-foot smokestack was a disaster waiting to happen, and on the afternoon of Monday, July 10, 1893, it did!

As can best be determined, the fire started in the cupola that surrounded and was flush with the top of the smoke stack. It started small enough, but there was a stiff breeze coming out of the northeast and, gradually, the flames circled around until the pillars of the cupola caught fire. By the time the top pillars were on fire, firemen had already reached the main roof of the building. The first attempt to get a hose to the first platform was by the use of an extension ladder from the southeast corner of the building, but was unsuccessful. Under orders of Acting Chief Murphy, men climbed the seventy feet up the tower from the outside by using cleats nailed to the side of the tower. The men took lengths of rope with them, but no ladders. When they finished their ascent to the first platform, they lowered their ropes and the process of pulling up hoses to the first platform began. While the firemen were valiantly attempting to put out the blaze, a crowd of about 30,000 fairgoers was forming around the building. A cheer broke out from the crowd when the first spurts of water burst from the hoses onto the fire above. It seemed to this awe-struck audience that the brave men of the Chicago Fire Department and Columbian Fire Department had the upper hand, but their cheers very suddenly turned to gasps of horror. The whole while that the men were planning their attack on the fire, it seemed, in retrospect, that the fire was already planning its revenge in the form of an almost-perfect death trap. In fact, it later became apparent that the firefighters' fates were sealed before the opening of the fair when the cold storage building's smoke stack was just an ugly piece of bare metal that extended 191 feet in the air. It was said that Daniel Burnham, Chief of Construction, did not like the stark contrast of the bare metal with the beauty of the "White City" and ordered that it be made to blend in with the surrounding buildings. The facade of wood and white painted staff that was erected around the stack did indeed blend well with the surrounding great buildings, but it also created a hollow gap between the façade and the pipe that extended below the main roof of the building. What the firefighters and the crowd didn't see were the burning embers falling through this gap and slowly igniting the material 70 feet below the firefighters.

For roughly ten minutes this hidden blaze was sealing the fate of many of the firefighters above. A small puff of smoke near their feet was the first indication to the brave souls above that something was terribly wrong. The firefighters on the roof could feel increased heat, but it wasn't coming only from above them anymore! As the firefighters on the roof sounded their warning, the crowd uttered a common cry of horror as flames erupted directly below the feet of the firefighters in the tower. It seemed to be only a split second between the initial burst of flame and when flames seemed to be pouring from between every pillar and even from the walls of the tower itself. The flames curled upwards surrounding the firefighters from both above and below them. Some in the crowed screamed, a women fainted, and one man went to his knees, lifting his arms upwards towards the sky to pray, as well as concentrating on looking upward and at the same time trying to avoid watching what was unfolding in front of him. The crowd was so dense at this point that no one could simply walk away and people were almost forced to witness what was quickly unfolding.

A silence fell over the crowd when a lone figure jumped from the seventy-foot ledge and frantically reached for the hose that extended down to the roof. He was only able to grab it with one hand, but managed to hold on. He slid down the hose into what seemed like a hopeless wall of fire that extended all the way down to the roof. He miraculously emerged from the flames with his clothes on fire, but still holding the hose. He made it to the roof and to the north side of the building, where he was lowered to the ground. He was John Davis of the fire company stationed on the Midway Plaisance. A split second can mean the difference between life and death in any fire, but almost a certainty in a fire of this magnitude. Unfortunately, firefighter Davis's comrades hesitated and the hose that could have been a lifeline for a select few was consumed by the flames and burned in half. Spectators could see the figure of Captain James Fitzpatrick, who was assigned to Engine Company 2 and was also Assistant Chief of Battalion 14 of the CFD. He seemed to be issuing orders to the men and one-by-one they started shimmying along the ledge of the tower to the north side, which seemed to offer a few more precious seconds from the fire's reach. There was another short-lived cheer as they all made the perilous journey to the north side of the tower. But the flames quickly looked to finish their morbid task. The men huddled closer and closer, attempting to avoid the heat of the oncoming flames. What happened next brought tears and cries from even the strongest in the crowd. There was an eerie calm that seemed to come

**Cold Storage Building at the Columbian
Exposition before the fire.** *Photograph
courtesy of the Fire Museum of Greater Chicago.*

across the men on the tower, and one man threw his arms around
the neck of another in what could be a final embrace. That started a
chain reaction of farewell words and hugs between the doomed men.
A rope was thrown out and fell almost to the roof, but even before
anyone could grab it, it was burnt in two. The firefighters on the roof
were frantically calling for ladders to be sent up from the ground,
but none came.

Without warning a figure took the seven-story jump to the roof
below, but the flame-ravaged wooden roof was no match for the weight
of the man and he fell through into a fiery inferno. Now it seemed the
only choice was to jump or burn and a second person took the fiery

Cold Storage Building during the tragedy.
*Photograph courtesy of the Fire Museum of
Greater Chicago.*

plunge and turned over and over until not landing on his feet, but
his head; he was killed instantly. Seeing the fate of the first of their
comrades, the rest of the group hesitated briefly, but the intensity of
the flames spurred them in their decision making.

In the crowd was Rev. Father O'Connor, a young Roman Catholic
priest from San Francisco. He had spent the day admiring the "White
City" and found himself a trapped spectator of this horror, like many
others. Still, while others were forcing themselves to look away or
becoming hysterical, Father O'Connor remained calm and knew in
his heart that the men were beyond physical help and appealed to

his heavenly Father. Father O'Connor forced himself to watch as each man jumped to his death, and as each man's body was still in the air, he raised his arms high and uttered the words, "Ego Te Absolvo!" To each and every man he administered the final sacrament of absolution. He didn't know their names or anything about how they lived their lives prior to this point. He also didn't know their religious beliefs, but the Catholic Church had ruled that Catholic or Protestant could be extended absolution and Father O'Connor had chosen, for obvious reasons, the shorter of the two forms of liturgy that could be used in times of extreme urgency. The ultimate result of the absolution, though, could only be determined by the spirit of the individual perishing.

Fireman W.P. Mahoney saw a comrade of his, named Bielenberg, pass out due to the heat of the flames. He picked up his friend and jumped for the rope. He managed to grab it and slowly both descended to the point that they both survived the initial impact on the roof, but Mahoney had broken both legs. He still managed to drag his friend to the north side of the building where they were both lowered by ladder to the ground.

There now remained only two firefighters left on the tower; one was Captain Fitzpatrick. He was trying to convince his comrade to go first, but to no avail. The Captain jumped to the only remaining rope, which had only about twenty feet left, and as he reached the burning end of the rope, swung himself hard to the north, avoiding the hottest of the flames. The last of those remaining attempted to duplicate the Captain's technique, but right at that moment, the tower could no longer support its own weight and it crashed into the burning inferno, taking the last unfortunate soul with it.

Chief Murphy had been on the burning roof for as long as he could, trying to do whatever he could, but was driven back by the intense heat. He had just reached the ground when Captain Fitzpatrick had fallen and called for Captain Kennedy of Company 5 and Hans Rehfeldt of the Hook and Ladder Company. The three shot up a ladder to the roof where Captain Fitzpatrick was laying. They raised him to his feet and tied a rope line securely under his arms and slowly lowered him to the ground. Many waiting hands grabbed the wounded firefighter and rushed him into a waiting ambulance.

Captain Fitzpatrick came from a fighting family and fought with his father and two brothers in the Battle of Gettysburg in the Civil War, where his father and one brother perished side by side. He himself was a veteran of over twenty battles, but he had fought his last fight on July 10, 1893. As the three men who pulled the Captain off the roof seemed to emerge from a wall of flames unharmed, the crowd burst into a round of applause and praise that could be heard all the way to the neighborhood of Englewood! As soon as the applause wore down, you could once again, however, hear the sobs and cries coming from the crowd. The building had, within the span of minutes, been reduced to a charred heap of rubble.

The last part of the building to fall was the grand east entrance. The painted metal (purportedly copper, but probably zinc) sculpture of Christopher Columbus holding the globe in his right hand had been pulled backward by the firefighters because it stood in the center of the entranceway blocking fire equipment. To either side of Columbus lounged the sculpture of a sphinx, with each catching fire, and its lathe skeleton being consumed. Finally, the entire building collapsed, burying Columbus in smoldering debris. The building used as a stable north of the cold storage building was completely consumed as well. The fire department managed to save the Color Building, paint shop, and the buildings outside the fair and directly across Cottage Grove were only scorched, although rumors of mass destruction had already sent insurance companies into a widespread panic. Rumors of scores of people perishing in the building were rampant. Many thought that there would be thirty to forty additional bodies found from the third and fourth floors because they housed the residences of missing Hercules employees. They were later located. Only their furniture was lost. The flames were finally under control at about 4 p.m. It seemed like an impossible task to keep the crowds under control and 800 Columbian Guards could not hold the throngs of on-lookers back. Forty-five U.S. soldiers with bayonets finally were called in to create a safe zone for firefighters to work in.

Now came the impossibly grotesque job of trying to identify the bodies of the fallen heroes. The first body was removed from the remains of the building about 5:30 p.m. and was nothing more than a charred stump. Bodies were removed at the rate of about one every fifteen minutes, until roughly eight bodies were recovered. Identification was very difficult and a coroner's jury was impaneled. One body wearing an electrician's belt was pulled out with a N.M. engraved in a belt buckle. This was later found to be the body of an electric lineman by the name of Norman M. Hartman. Once night had fallen, Chief Murphy suspended any further searches until the following day.

While human beings can never be replaced and the cost of the loss of life impossible to place a number on, there were plenty of monetary losses involved in the burning of the Cold Storage building. It was estimated that every state in the Union and every foreign government in attendance had sustained substantial losses. Most of the commodities lost were beer, wine, ales, and last year's fruit that was to be entered into competition. The Spanish government lost an estimated $20,000 worth of fine wines and liquor, and the Lowney Company of Boston lost thousands of dollars in chocolate. All of the restaurants at the fair received their ice from the building, although not everyone was displeased with the Hercules Co. no longer supplying ice, because many believed that their price of $4 per ton was ridiculously high-priced and of a very poor "spongy" quality. Ice could be procured from outside companies for about $2.50 per ton or about a 40 percent savings in cost. While it would be quite some time before the total cost of the tragedy in both human and monetary loss could be calculated, the first legal judgment against the Hercules Iron Works was entered in the Cook County Superior Court for $15,498 in favor of Malek A. Toring before the flames of the building were completely extinguished!

The last body was taken out of the building at 5 p.m. on Tuesday, July 11th, although there was a short time when 10 dressed sheep were found and mistaken for human remains. They were quickly identified as sheep, but not before the newspapers had published the report.

The clearing away of the debris of the building was in the hands of Daniel Burnham, who promised to put 200 workers on the task. On July 12th, a committee was formed by the city council to investigate the remaining buildings for possible fire hazards. Marshal Murphy of the Fair Fire Department and alderman Madden, who headed up the committee, were accompanied by aldermen Martin, Noble, Kerr, and Wadsworth to tour the buildings of the fair looking to make fire safety recommendations. (Chicago has not had a great history with fires and that is one of the reasons the Cook County Electrical Code is one of the strictest in the nation.) Marshal Murphy was not pleased with many of the public rooftop observation areas located throughout the park. In particular, he was not pleased with the roof of the Manufacturer's and Liberal Arts Building (the largest of the expo buildings)—1,000 to 1,500 people on the rooftop observation area was not unheard of and there were no stairs leading off the roof. The only access up and down was by four elevators capable of holding a maximum of fifteen passengers at a time and each trip taking between three to four minutes. It doesn't take long to see how quickly once an alarm sounded that a stampede and death trap situation would develop.

Original sketch of the Columbus statue from the Cold Storage Building fire by artist Kimberly MacAulay.

Unidentified/Unclaimed Victim Not Accounted For on the Official Monument

A fund was established and collected by a committee appointed by President Higinbotham of the World's Fair and Mayor Harrison to meet the needs, immediate and future, of the beneficiaries of the fallen heroes. Donations poured in, and Sunday, July 16th, was deemed Heroes Day at the Fair. All gate proceeds on that date were to be used to pay for the funerals of all those who had lost their lives. By the end of August, the total in the fund exceeded $100,000, making it one of the largest of its kind, although distribution rules had not yet been setup. If divided equally among the thirty-five families entitled, it would have amounted to roughly $2,800 per family, although it was agreed that each family's situation should be looked at individually and given money according to each of their needs.

July 14th was the day most of the fire heroes were laid to rest and the seven bodies that were claimed (but not distinguished from one another) were laid to rest at Oakwoods Cemetery next to where the planned monument to all of the victims was to be placed in the near future. The *Chicago Tribune* reported on July 14th that all of the bodies were matched to a claiming family or person and described the burials of the Unidentified as such:

> At 1:30 o'clock today the funeral cortege of the unidentified persons will start from the engine house at Forty-Sixth Street and Cottage Grove Avenue. Carriages will be in readiness for all those who wish to pay their last respects to the memory of the unknown dead. Yesterday relatives of the missing men, Breen, Garvey and Cahill, called upon Father Hishen of the Holy Cross Church in Woodlawn and asked him to say the prayers over the dead. He gave a ready consent and tomorrow the funeral procession will stop on its way to Oakwoods Cemetery and the mourners will enter the chapel at Sixty-Sixth Street and Maryland Avenue, where prayers will be said. Should any Protestant friends of the missing men desire to have services held over the remains, special arrangements will be made to have these conducted in the engine house before the start for the grave. The proprietors of Oakwoods have donated a lot for the burial of these unidentified dead and this was selected yesterday by D.H. Burnham.

It was in a July 21st edition of the *Chicago Tribune* where I found a small blurb about one of the bodies being buried, but never claimed. There was no other mention anywhere of a truly unknown victim of the fire, so I had to do a small investigation of my own. By all accounts, the claimed victims amounted to fifteen individuals. The fifteen individuals consisted of four regular members of the Chicago Fire Department, eight members of the Columbian Fire Department, and three civilians. I put together a list of the fallen with the job or position that they held at the time of the fire, age, death certificate number, and the cemetery in which they were laid to rest. When the numbers shook out, there should have only been six bodies buried at Oakwoods Cemetery, when there were actually seven! I confirmed the burials with the Oakwoods Cemetery Office and they provided me with a diagram of the monument and locations of the seven bodies buried around the Granite Monument listing all of the names of the victims, whether they were firemen or not. The following is the list of names and burial locations, with those buried at Oakwoods listed last:

1. Captain James Fitzpatrick, Engine Co. 2 and Assistant Chief of Battalion 14, Chicago Fire Department, age 54, death certificate #4802, St. James of the Sag Cemetery.
2. Ralph H. Drummond, Superintendent of the Harter Electric Company, age 27, death certificate #3345, Rosehill Cemetery.

3. William H. Denning, World's Fair Hook and Ladder #8, age 33, death certificate #3346, Calvary Cemetery, Evanston, IL.
4. Lt. John H. Freeman, World's Fair Engine Co. 1, age 45, death certificate #4923, Springfield, IL.
5. John C. McBride, Driver, World's Fair Engine Co. 8, age 33, death certificate #12697, Chatsworth, IL.

The monument erected to the victims of the Cold Storage Fire at Oakwoods Cemetery in Chicago, IL.

6. Louis J. Frank, Fireman, World's Fair Engine Co. 2, age 30, death certificate #4924, Concordia Cemetery, Forest Park, IL.
7. Lt. Charles W. Purvis, Truckman Hook and Ladder #4 Chicago Fire Department, Lt. World's Fair Engine Co. 4, age 28, death certificate #14392, Mount Olivet Cemetery.

8. Paul W. Schroeder, Driver, World's Fair Departmen Engine Co. 2, age 22, death certificate #16975, Waldheim Cemetery.
9. John A. Smith, Driver, World's Fair Department Engine Co. 2, age 26, death certificate #16976, Calvary Cemetery, Evanston, IL.
10. Captain James A. Garvey, Engine Co. 1, Chicago Fire Department, age 32, death certificate #5826, Oakwoods Cemetery Memorial.
11. Norman M. Hartman, Electric Light Lineman, age 24, death certificate #7110, Oakwoods Cemetery Memorial.
12. John Cahill, Truckman, World's Fair Department Engine Co. 8, age 37, death certificate #2372, Oakwoods Cemetery Memorial.
13. Phillip J. Breen, Truckman, World's Fair Department Chemical Engine Co. 14, age 26, death certificate #955, Oakwoods Cemetery Memorial.
14. Bernard Murphy, Boilermaker, age 25, death certificate #11640, Oakwoods Cemetery Memorial.
15. Captain Burton E. Page, Lt. Truck Number 15, Chicago Fire Department, age 33, death certificate #14391, Oakwoods Cemetery Memorial.
16. Unidentified / Unclaimed victim, Oakwoods Cemetery Memorial.

There are only six names associated with the seven burials at the Oakwoods Memorial with no mention of an unknown victim. The six are: Captain James A. Garvey, Norman M. Hartman, Captain Burton E. Page, John Cahill, Phillip Breen, Bernard Murphy, and one unknown.

There were a number of possible identities of the unknown and unclaimed victim, and they were:

1. A fire truck driver by the name of M. McQuade reported missing on July 11th.
2. A Mr. Fowler (first name unknown) who was employed by the Cold Storage Building reported missing on July 11th.
3. A Robert Blenhuber who was a capitalist from Marquette, MI reported missing whom I did find living in the 1940 Census still residing in Marquette.
4. H.W. Allen, living at 428 Hancock Street in Sandusky, OH, who was reported missing by his wife eleven days after the fire.
5. A foreman of painters named Henry Ceduldid.

No positive identification or claim was ever made of the seventh unidentified victim buried under the monument at Oakwoods Cemetery. Of course, identification of victims was much more difficult before the evolution of modern forensic techniques and they didn't have the technology that is available to us today, so it might make for an interesting archeological project for the descendants of the sixteenth official victim of the fire.

RELIC OF THE FIRE STILL SURVIVES

Shortly after the debris of the Cold Storage Building had been cleared away, the owner of the twelve-foot metal statue of Columbus wanted to donate it to the Fire Department to be used as the Official Monument in Oakwoods Cemetery to honor those of the fallen. The owner, William Hardy Mullins of Salem, Ohio, thought it to be a fitting tribute. The Statue, however, violated Oakwoods' monument policy and the monument became what is currently in place. Just to the southwest of the Oakwoods Memorial Chapel is a modest granite stone emblazoned with a single granite fire helmet and listing all fifteen known victims of the fire, even though only six known victims and one unknown victim (not referenced on the monument or on cemetery records) are buried in Section D, Division 4, Lot 16 with the City of Chicago listed as the owner of the lot.

I was elated to find out that, while the Christopher Columbus Statue was not able to be used as the official monument, it was still presented to Chief Joseph Kenyon of the 12th Battalion by the owner, Mr. Mullins, at the close of the Columbian Exposition. It was erected in front of Engine Co. 51's Quarters at 6345 S. Wentworth Avenue in memory of the fallen heroes of the Cold Storage Fire. Engine 51 was probably selected as the recipient because it was Battalion Headquarters and Chief Kenyon that had actually helped fight the blaze. After Engine Co. 51 closed its doors, the statue was moved to the Fire Department Maintenance Shops. The statue was refurbished, repainted, and put on display at City Hall in October of 1993. Later, it was moved to the 9-1-1 Center on Madison Street and was, finally, in October 2001, placed in its current location of honor.

I am in the process of attempting to locate as many artifacts from the Columbian Exposition that still exist and was very happy when I located the original twelve-foot metal statue of Christopher Columbus at 5218 S. Western Avenue which was the former home of Chicago Fire Department Engine Co. 123, but is the current home of the Fire Museum of Greater Chicago. The museum is run by former and current members of the Chicago Fire Department and operates strictly on donations.

The Jackson Park Fieldhouse at 64th and Stony Island Avenue is located roughly where the Cold Storage Building would have stood in 1893.

I had the opportunity to meet three of the volunteers who help to run the museum and to see the Columbus statue up close. It was amazing to be in the presence of something with such historical significance and I almost wished it could talk, so that I could ask it questions about the fire. Jack Connors invited me to the museum and introduced me to the Fire Chaplain, Father John McNalis, and the Vice President of the museum, Frank McMenamin. What a wonderful, passionate group of firefighters with a wealth of knowledge about the history of the Chicago Fire Department. I believe that the heroes who lost their lives in the Cold Storage Fire, and all of the heroes of the Chicago Fire Department, would be proud of what they are accomplishing with the help of the many volunteers from the fire service past and present. I owe them a debt of gratitude for helping me with much of the research for this chapter of the book.

Columbus statue from the east entrance of the Cold Storage Building on display at the Fire Museum of Greater Chicago.

Current home of the Fire Museum of Greater Chicago, 5218 S. Western Avenue, Chicago, IL.

The Devil, The White City,
William Green, and
The Cook County Sheriff

Since Erik Larson's book, *The Devil in The White City*, Herman Webster Mudgett, alias Dr. H.H. Holmes, has been forever linked with the 1893 Chicago World's Columbian Exposition and his "murder castle" at 701-703 63rd Street in Chicago's Englewood neighborhood.

The castle, from the outside, was much like many of the other small hotels that had sprung up around Chicago shortly before the exposition to accommodate the many out-of-town visitors to the fair, but Mudgett's had one very distinct difference. The second floor of Mudgett's "hotel" was set up as a killing floor. A virtual maze, it included rooms equipped with gas lines that Mudgett could turn on and off to asphyxiate guests at will. There was a chute that ran from the second floor to the basement where a body could be quickly transported and cremated in the special high-heat furnace that he had installed.

Mudgett had made his more or less permanent move to Chicago as early as 1884 or 1885, but may have made short trips back and forth prior

**Original sketch of
Herman Webster
Mudgett, a.k.a. H.H.
Holmes, by artist
Kimberly MacAulay.**

to that. Dubbed "America's First Serial Killer" by popular media, he didn't quite fit the typical mold of a serial killer. Most serial killers do not have the wherewithal to complete a project that takes sustained mental effort, such as earning an advanced academic degree. Mudgett actually graduated from the University of Michigan Medical School in June of 1884. In addition, most serial killers are driven by an uncontrollable need or strong desire to kill. I have been fascinated by Mudgett (as a former criminal investigator) for many years and have researched much of his exploits while in Chicago, and from what I gather, Mudgett seems to me to be more driven by greed and ego, while displaying classic sociopathic traits that make killing someone as easy as you and I take out the garbage. If he could find a way to make money, and somebody had to die in the process, then that was how it had to be. If someone got in the way of his plans, knew too much, or was more trouble to keep around than they were worth to him, then they had to be eliminated. Oh, and if he could make money off the body by having it stripped of its flesh and the skeleton sold to local colleges, then all the better.

While there has been much research done on the subject of Herman Webster Mudgett and his victims, I became interested in researching what types of associations Mudgett formed while in Chicago and in following some of his many con games to see what sort of information might come of it. Anyone who has ever tried to follow Holmes and his exploits (and I will refer to Mudgett as Holmes from here on out) knows what type of monumental headache can develop as a result. Holmes had an untold number of aliases and it is known that he was lying whenever his lips were moving. Of course, mixed with those lies were half truths, deceptions, and misdirections. Holmes was a master con artist. I have encountered persons with similar personality traits to Holmes while an investigator, but none that came close to the level of audacity, abandon, and pure artistry of deceit that came naturally to Holmes. I know that may sound similar to a compliment, but that could not be further from the truth. Holmes was in a class of criminal degenerate all his own.

Holmes was very well known for purchasing items for sale in his murder castle on credit and generally had a worthless promissory note signed, usually by either one of his own aliases or by an unwitting victim of his con. Many times it was hard to figure out who was who. One such case caught my attention in the summer of 2011 when I was doing a survey of Cook County Chancery cases at the Cook County Archives. I was attempting to review old cases that may have involved Holmes, his associates, and many of his aliases. I found that he had been listed as a defendant numerous times, but only once (under the name of Holmes) as a plaintiff! It fascinated me that Holmes was using the same Justice system that he so often mocked. It seemed that Holmes was suing J. L. Connor for non-payment on a promissory note.

The case was filed on September 28, 1891, and it seems that J.L. Connor was actually later one of his confirmed victims, Julia Connor. The note was written on the Englewood Bank and it was payable to H.H. Holmes in the amount of $1,942.28 twelve months from the date of issue, which was September 13, 1890. That fact alone was not very remarkable because Holmes would many times pay employees (Julia was technically an employee of his), but then get the money back (plus some) by telling them that they were investing in a business of his and that they would become part owner. What interested me was that in one of the pages of the complaint, the purpose for the promissory note was listed. Many times the purpose of the note was not laid out specifically in the remaining paperwork of the case, and oftentimes, is just listed as "for goods and/or services rendered." In this case, it stipulated that the money was for the rent of an upstairs office space in the murder castle for the use of William Green and Henry Rogers doing business as "William Green & Co."

Holmes was not known to keep legitimate business concerns in the building in general and especially not on the upper floors. Why would Julia Connor be paying the rent for William Green & Co.? Was the William Green & Co. a legitimate business and Holmes merely using their name as an excuse as to why Julia Connor owed him the money or was the William & Green Co. another make-believe company of Holmes' used to swindle even more hapless souls?

My search for the William Green & Co. turned up a listing for a corporation that was headed up by a William Green and Henry Rogers.

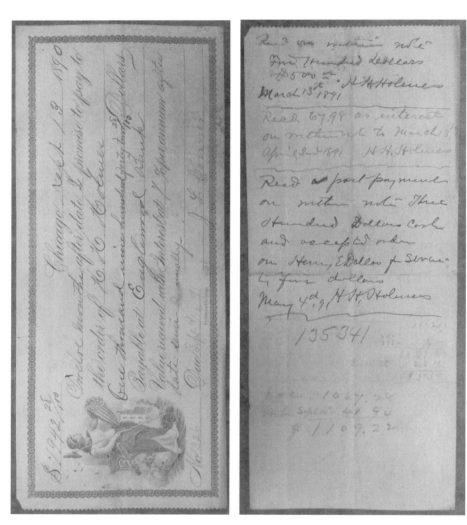

Photograph of promissory note bearing the signature of H.H. Holmes supposedly presented to Holmes by future victim Julia Connor for the rent of William Green & Co. at the "Murder Castle."

I found an article in the *Chicago Tribune*, dated October 9, 1892, that mentioned Henry Rogers, from Appleton, Wisconsin, purchasing a warehouse for $50,000 for the use of the William Green & Co. for cement and general warehousing business. The address of the warehouse was 544-554 North Water Street and the newspaper describes the location as such:

The warehouse is located on North Water Street, 1,600 feet east of St. Clair Street, and running to the river, is a five-story and basement brick building of mill construction, 100 x 150 feet in size, with a two-story brick addition in the rear. The building has been owned and occupied successively by the Rathbone, Sard & Co., the Western Refrigerating Company, and the Fuller & Warren Company. The ground, which is 120 feet by 196 feet on the east line, by 208 feet on the west line, with a Chicago and Northwestern railway switch in the front and a dock in the rear, is owned by the Chicago Dock and Canal Company, and has been leased to Mr. Rogers for a term of sixty two years.

The deal was negotiated by William A. Bond & Co. and, as a side note, Holmes used the alias A. Bond or Alexander Bond when swindling victims Minnie and Anna Williams from Texas.

WILLIAM GREEN...SWINDLER IN HIS OWN RIGHT, HOLMES CONFEDERATE OR HOLMES ALIAS?

While attempting to gain more information on William Green and his business dealings in Chicago, I came across information in the *Chicago Tribune* as well as via the Cook County Clerk of the Circuit Court Archives. It seems that a William Green, a.k.a, Francis W. Green, was being looked at by authorities for swindling a young man, referred to as "a farmer boy" by the *Chicago Daily Tribune* on October 12, 1893. The farmer boy's name was Gerard J. Riddle or "Riddell," according to court documents. The complaint filed by Riddell on October 7, 1893, advised that Riddell was a native of England and had met the "son" of William Green while a student of the science of farming at Mount St. Mary's College near Chesterfield, Derbyshire, England, in November or December of 1892. Riddell stated that William Green's son had been admitted to holy orders in the Order of Jesuits of the Holy Catholic Church and he introduced Riddell to his father, William Green, a.k.a Francis W. Green.

Riddell told Green about his desire to emigrate to America and engage in the business of farming there. Riddell then introduced Green to his mother and father and Green convinced Riddell's parents that the business of farming was a very lucrative one in America and that Green could handle the business affairs side of Riddell's venture overseas. Riddell's parents entrusted Green with 150 pounds sterling, which was equivalent to approximately $750. William Green booked passage for himself and Riddell in the month of April for their trip to America and Riddell met William Green in Liverpool to embark on the journey.

I traced Gerard Riddell and William Green to a ship manifest from the S.S. *Teutonic* of the White Star Line. This is where the story starts to get shaky. I did find Gerard J. "Reddell," 31, as well as William Green, 28, on the ship manifest arriving in New York on April 27, 1893. There was, however, also a Frank Green, 29 (William's alias was Francis Green), as well as a Sir Edw. Green, 43, his wife "Lady" Green, 39, and their maid, Ellen Marshall, 28. What doesn't make sense is the fact that Gerard Riddell supposedly met William Green's son while a student at Mount St. Mary's College in 1892. Mount St. Mary's is in fact a college for students 11-18 years of age and has been since 1842. The oldest Gerard Riddell would have been in 1893 would have been 19 years of age. What's more, William Green was supposed to have been the father of a classmate of Gerard Riddell, which would have meant that William Green would have more than likely been considerably older than Riddell. On the ship manifest, Gerard "Redell" is listed as 31 years of age (the same age Holmes would have been at the time). William Green and Frank Green were 28 and 29 respectively, which would make them younger than Gerard Riddell. Judging from past research of Holmes, I can only conclude that Riddell (probably no more than 18 to 20 years old at the time) never made it out of England alive. I am of the opinion that Holmes simply assumed the identity of Riddell for the trip back and William Green and Francis Green were confederates of Holmes (whether or not the Green names were real or aliases, I have been unable to determine). One interesting fact was that William Green and Frank, or Francis, Green were supposedly from England, but on the ship manifest, it listed their nation of origin as "U.S.A."!

The complaint by Riddell, or "Holmes," continues by saying that Riddell accompanied Green to Chicago and Green had rented a house in Englewood where he furnished said house and charged Riddell $20 per week for rent, which was paid out of the money entrusted to Green by Riddell's parents. Shortly after coming to Chicago, Green supposedly had received information about a farm near Custer Park in Will County consisting of 120 acres and wrote to Riddell's parents requesting that they send $7,000 in order to purchase the farm for Riddell. The parents had sent a draft for 1,400 pounds, which was roughly $7,000, made out to the order of Gerard Riddell. Riddell endorsed the draft and Green converted the order to cash and deposited that cash in a safety deposit box at the National Safe Deposit Company in Chicago. Green allegedly told Riddell that the farm cost $4,700 when in fact, as much as Riddell could determine, the farm only cost $3,700 and that Green had pocketed $1,000 for himself. When challenged, Green agreed to pay back $500 to Riddell with a note signed by one Rogers, and being ignorant of business matters, signed a receipt to Green for the $500 guaranteed by "Rogers." Soon after this, Green again contacted Riddell's parents in England, requesting that they send an additional $5,000 in order to purchase further lands adjacent to the current farm and that it would be advantageous for Riddell. Riddell's parents again sent a $5,000 draft made out to Riddell, which Riddell again signed over to Green. (Could Riddell again be so gullible as to sign over an additional $5,000 to Green given his track record so far?) At this point, Green converts the money into currency and deposits it in the same safety deposit box. Riddell stated that roughly $12,000 was entrusted to Green from the time of their arrival to the U.S. for the expenses of Riddell and the purchase of various properties, which Riddell had supposedly never seen paperwork for. When Riddell approached Green asking for an accounting of the money, Green stated that the balance of the account minus Riddell's expenses was $6,700, although Green could not provide documentation for this and Riddell did not have any knowledge of expenditures, other than Green's statements and the small amounts of money that Riddell would apply for to cover minor living expenses. Green took Riddell to the safety deposit box at the National Safe Deposit Company and showed him the inside of the box, which contained $6,700 in bank notes and other instruments. He provided Riddell with access and a key to the box shortly before Riddell stated he was going on a trip to Denver, Colorado. Riddell locked the box, which he believed contained $6,700 and left on a train bound for Denver within the next hour. Riddell returned on September 22, 1893, and did not return to the safety deposit box until September 28th. When Riddell opened the box, it contained notes amounting to $700 and there was $6,000 missing.

Riddell had been out of town for three weeks and stated that Green had opened a secret box at the Home Safety Deposit Vault Company and that Riddle was sure that the missing $6,000 or part thereof would be in this "secret" box. Riddle requested in his complaint that injunctions be ordered by the court to freeze Green's access to his safety deposit boxes until the court could order an accounting based on Riddles accusations of fraud by William Green. Riddle also claimed that he had acquired knowledge that Green had purchased a train ticket to New York in order to be able to board the S.S. *Majestic* to Liverpool, England, which was scheduled to depart on October 11, 1893.

I thought that it was unlikely that as gullible as Riddell seemed to be that he somehow had acquired information about a secret safety deposit box and also was aware of Green's travel (escape) plans to England, including ship and departure date. It seemed to me to be more of a case of "no honor among thieves" and that somehow the arrangement between Green and Holmes had gone bad. Keep in mind that I am still unsure of who was who. Was "Green" another name for Holmes and Riddell one of Holmes's confederates or vice versa? Keep in mind that I do believe that there was originally an actual Gerard J. Riddell and that he had been killed prior to leaving England and the two conspirators were defrauding Riddell's parents of the money they thought they were sending to their son, and then one of the conspirators tried to make off with all the loot, forcing the other to again take the identity of Gerard Riddell in order to start legal paperwork to freeze access to various safety deposit boxes. According to the *Chicago Tribune*, Green was arrested in Chicago on October 7, 1893, in response to Riddell's complaint. Green, however, made bail and convinced his bail bondsman that he was indeed going to England in a couple of days, but promised to return for the court proceedings. The newspaper stated that he never returned. Since Green admitted to the authorities that he was intending to leave the country, he would not have been induced to use an alias when traveling. There were no listings of any William Green arriving in the U.K. from New York in either October or November of 1893! I have a hunch that the "Englishman, William Green" never quite made it out of Chicago.

In an interesting turn of events, it appeared, according to court paperwork, that Riddell retained the services of attorney Henry O' Herigan in place of his first attorney, Robert Mather, and this new attorney filed to have the entire case dismissed, as well as all injunctions dismissed on behalf of Riddell. It appears that Riddle may have gotten what he wanted and no longer needed the assistance of our judicial system. There are parts of Holmes' "confession" that I believe may point to the fate of "William Green."

LINKS TO HOLMES'S "CONFESSION"

Holmes was paid by William Randolph Hearst to write a confession to be published in Hearst's newspapers while Holmes was a guest of Moyamensing Prison in Philadelphia. Holmes signed the confession on April 9, 1896. Much of this confession was an outright lie and many persons he claimed to have killed were later found to be alive; many of the names were made up or names of others who he had come across in some of his "business" dealings, and many who were counted as living were actually his victims. One must take much of the confession with a grain of salt, but being a former investigator myself, I understand how many confessions or statements by a defendant are a mixture of truth and lies, with the truth usually sprinkled in to help a story flow better and assist the liar in trying to recreate the story later. Lies are hard to remember, but the truth is seldom forgotten. One of the papers that ran the confession was the *Philadelphia Inquirer* and I thought it was quite interesting that Holmes included an account, albeit a half-truth Holmesian account, of his dealings with William Green and Henry Rogers.

In his confession, Holmes states:

In 1891 I associated myself in business with a young Englishman, whose name I am more than willing to publish to the world, but I am advised it could not be published on my unsupported statement, who by his own admission, had been guilty of all other forms of wrongdoing, save murder and presumably of that as well. To manipulate certain real estate securities we held so as to have them secure us a good commercial rating was an easy matter for him and he was equally able to interest certain English capitalists in patents so that for a time it seemed that in the near future our greatest concern would be how to dispose of the money that seemed about to be showered upon us. By an unforeseen occurrence our rating was destroyed and it became necessary to at once raise a large sum and this was done by my partner enticing to Chicago a wealthy banker named Rogers from a North Wisconsin town in such a manner that he could have left no intelligence with whom his business was to be. To cause him to go to the castle and within the secret room under the pretense that our patents were there was easily brought about, more so to force him to sign checks and drafts for seventy thousand dollars, which we had prepared. At first he refused to do so, stating that his liberty that we offered him in exchange would be useless to him without his money, that, he was too old to again hope to make another fortune. Finally, by alternately starving him and nauseating him with the gas he was made to sign the securities, all of which were converted into money and by my partner's skill as a forger in such a manner as to leave no trace of their having passed through our hands. I waited with much curiosity to see what propositions my partner would advance for the disposal of our prisoner, as I well knew he, no more than I, contemplated giving him his liberty. My partner evidently waited with equal expectancy for me to suggest what should be done, and I finally made preparation to allow him to leave the building, thus forcing him to suggest that he be killed. I would only consent to this upon the condition that he should administer the chloroform, and leave me to dispose of the body as my part of the work. In this way I was enabled to keep him in ignorance of my dealings with the medical college agent. That evening this large sum of money was equally divided between us, and my partner went to the Palmer House, where he was well known, and passed the night at cards with three other men.

There is only one problem with this part of his confession…Henry Rogers was never murdered by Green or Holmes. In fact, he was being sued by numerous creditors of the William Green & Co. for materials that were ordered, but never paid for or used in legitimate business practices. One of those orders was for a large amount of Portland cement. Call me silly, but anytime you have a murderer with access to large amounts of cement and private access to the Chicago River, it usually adds up to an easy way of disposing of bodies or body parts. It also makes me think, based on other half truths contained in his several confessions published by various newspapers of the time that the plight of Henry Rogers was actually that of "William Green" of the William Green & Co. and not that of Rogers himself. Rogers actually passed away on July 27, 1896, a little less than three months after Holmes was executed by hanging at Moyamensing Prison on May 8, 1896, for the murder of Benjamin Pitezel. According to his death certificate, he was a warehouseman and died at the Plaza Hotel of bladder cancer. He was buried in Graceland Cemetery in Chicago. His wife, Cremora, continued on at 1947 Deming Place (now 437 Deming after the Chicago re-numbering of 1909), moved in with her daughter and son-in-law, Florence and Frank Pietsch, around 1910 at 2820 N. Lakeview Avenue, and died in Buffalo, New York, on March 1, 1919. She is buried next to her husband at Graceland Cemetery.

HENRY J. ROGERS, HISTORICALLY SIGNIFICANT PATSY

It seemed with Holmes that whenever he developed a scheme or "business venture" he always involved one true victim who had access to money. After all, what kind of con-man would you be if the person you were spending valuable con-time on had no money? He would very often form a company or venture with one or two actual people who had access to money, coupled with imaginary people who ended up being Holmes's aliases, former dupes, or murder victims. That is another reason why the William Green & Co. smells like another Holmes scheme.

A discussion of Henry J. Rogers can begin at the Hearthstone Historic House Museum in Appleton, Wisconsin. The house, located at 625 Prospect Avenue, was originally built in 1882 by Henry J. Rogers as a showplace for his wife, Cremora, and daughter, Florence (Kitty). Rogers had enlisted the skill of architect William Waters who ironically was also the architect for the Wisconsin Building at the 1893 World's Columbian Exposition in Chicago! The house is approximately 9,000 square feet and boasts nine fireplaces, which is where it received its current name "Hearthstone" when it was converted to the Hearthstone restaurant in the 1930s after changing owners nine times. Rogers was the manager of the Appleton Pulp and Paper Mill and came up with the idea of using the Fox River to not only light his mill, but also to generate electricity for his home. He had contacted H.E. Jacobs, a representative of the Western Edison Light Company, in July of 1882, and a dynamo was placed in the beater room of the Appleton Pulp and Paper Mill. On September 30, 1882, history was made when the single hydroelectric plant, using Thomas Edison technology powered three separate buildings: the Appleton Pulp and Paper Mill, Kimberly-Clark's Vulcan Mill, and Rogers' residence. The home still employs many of the original Edison switches and was placed on the National Register of Historic Places on December 2, 1974. It may be the last surviving example of original wiring and fixtures in their original location from the dawn of the electrical age. It was Rogers, and investors A.L. Smith, H.D. Smith, and Charles Beveridge, who later retained the rights to operate this first hydroelectric plant, which led to the incorporation of the Appleton Edison Electric Company in 1890.

Rogers and his family lived in the residence for about eleven years until they moved to Chicago in the year of the Columbian Exposition.

THE ABC COPIER CO., THOMAS B. BRYAN, COMMISSIONER-AT-LARGE OF "THE WHITE CITY," AND THE COOK COUNTY SHERIFF

The names and the date (1891) may have been the only truths contained in Holmes's confession concerning William Green and Henry Rogers. Before the 1893 Gerard J. Riddell fiasco, I mentioned that I had first come across the names William Green and Henry Rogers as tenants in the "murder castle" in 1891, according to court documents filed by Holmes himself (it was his signature on the promissory note), when he was suing one of his future victims, Julia Connor. The William Green & Co. also figured into the short history of the ABC Copier Co., which has been referred to as one of Holmes's almost "legitimate" ventures. Actually, the beginnings of the ABC Copier Co. in Chicago go back to 1890 and involve not H.H. Holmes, but none other than Thomas Barbour Bryan. Bryan was born in Virginia in 1828 and graduated from Harvard University Law School in 1848. He came to Chicago in 1852 and began purchasing quite a good amount of real estate along Michigan Avenue and State Street and also the land that Graceland Cemetery currently stands on. He lost an estimated $500,000 in real estate during the Chicago Fire of 1871. In 1856, he moved his residence to a small village about twenty miles west of Chicago called Cottage Hill. He was perplexed by the fact that there was no "cottage" and no "hill" there, so he planted an estimated 1,000 trees, many of them elm trees, and other plants at his home he called "Byrd's Nest" because of his wife's maiden name, Jennie Byrd Page. In fact, it is said that he gave Cottage Hill its new name, Elmhurst—the elm being a good number of the trees that he had planted with the old Saxon word "hurst" meaning planting or seedtime.

Mr. Bryan was the head of the committee that traveled to Washington, D.C. to lobby for Chicago to be chosen as the location for the 1893 World's Columbian Exposition and at one time was credited with coming up with the idea of the "World's Fair" in Chicago, but he gave that credit to a newspaperman, J.W. Scott. He was given the title Commissioner-at-Large of the World's Columbian Exposition and was also the Vice President of the World's Congress Auxiliary of the Fair that met at the building that is now the Art Institute of Chicago. As Commissioner-at-Large, Bryan traveled throughout Europe, visiting with many crowned heads of state as well as securing (as a Protestant no less) a personal meeting with Pope Leo XIII while in Rome and being presented with a personal letter from the Pope, which fully endorsed the World's Columbian Exposition and suggested that the entire world give it its full support!

In the fall of 1890, shortly after the push for a Chicago World's Fair had begun, Thomas Bryan was approached by a young Englishman named Frederick George Nind. Bryan stated that he knew Nind to be an upstanding young man and trustworthy. Nind had come to him to ask for his monetary assistance in buying what Bryan described as a "European" patent called the A.B.C. Copier Company. Because Bryane knew Nind to be "honest and deserving young man," he loaned him several thousand dollars and took the patent as security for a loan. Bryan stated that he had no connection to the business, but that Nind had told him that he would repay Bryan his money when he found someone to purchase the patent. The A.B.C. Copier Company was incorporated on October 16, 1890, by Thomas B. Bryan, F.G. Nind, and J.D. Vandercook. About a year later, Nind introduced H.H. Holmes to Bryan. Bryan stated that he was unimpressed by Holmes, but that he stated that he would be interested in purchasing Bryan's half of the business. Holmes presented Bryan a note endorsed by a Mary Durkee—obviously a fictitious name combining the names of Kate Durkee from Omaha and Mary Kelly from Chicago. Kelly was a typist and notary for Holmes while Kate Durkee had been instrumental in placing Holmes' real estate in her name in order to hide his interest in it. Bryan soon found out the note was worthless and the business was sold through court proceedings to satisfy Bryan's claim against Holmes.

Nind's account seems to be slightly different in that Nind claims that he purchased the patent for the A.B.C. Copier Company in London and had asked Bryan if he would be interested in going into business with him. It was then that Bryan bought into his half of the business. Nind believed that the woman who endorsed the $9,000 note to Bryan, in order to buy the business, was Kate Durkee from Omaha. Once Holmes "purchased" his half of the business from Bryan using a bogus note, Nind went to New York and established an eastern agency of the company in conjunction with Henry Bainbridge & Co. and F.W. Devee & Co. Upon Nind's return to Chicago, Holmes told Nind that the company was in trouble and he introduced Nind to his attorney, Wharton Plummer, who stated that he represented parties who were willing to buy out the troubled business and promise $25,000 worth of the manufactured products to Holmes and Nind. Nind agreed and basically put Plummer in full ownership of the company and Nind never saw a dime.

There is the story out there that the A.B.C. Copier Co. duped another company out of a large quantity of gasoline. According to Mary Kelly, an actual person and once thought to be just another alias for Kate Durkee, it was the William Green & Co. that was caught holding the bag after a large purchase of glycerine (industrial lubricant), not gasoline. She worked for Holmes at the A.B.C Copier Co., room 720 of the Monon Building at 320-326 S. Dearborn, and after the business closed, she followed Holmes to his newest business venture, The Chicago Intermediate Company in room 93 of the sixth floor of the Illinois Bank Building at 115 S. Dearborn. She said that the company would sell anything or provide any service to anyone for a fee. It was incorporated as a business "to investigate and report upon the financial standing of persons and corporations." (Holmes may have actually had a sense of humor!)

Holmes convinced Kelly that she would benefit in her career as a secretary by becoming a notary public. She remembered notarizing a large amount of documents for Holmes, supposedly signed by many different individuals. She had a feeling that there was something underhanded going on, but never confronted Holmes on the subject (lucky for her). In fact, she was quoted by the *Chicago Tribune* as saying she wouldn't be surprised to see her name as one of the officers of the Chicago Intermediate Company. In reality, Holmes incorporated the business under the names of Mary Durkee. (Mary Kelly was half right.)

After the glycerine incident, the William Green & Co. (probably only Henry Rogers, since Green was either an alias of Holmes or a con-man in his own right) filed a lawsuit against the A.B.C. Copier Co., as well as the persons of Thomas B. Bryan, his brother Charles P. Bryan, Hiram S. Campbell (Holmes or Ben Pitezel alias), Kate Durkee, and Julia L. Connor. Probably not a coincidence, but the attorneys on record representing the William Green & Co. was the firm of Tenney, Church & Coffeen who were the same attorneys that Holmes was using to sue Julia Connor, and both suits (Green vs. ABC) and (Holmes vs. Connor) were filed almost simultaneously. Of course, the A.B.C Copier Co. was using their Vice President, attorney Wharton Plummer, as their defense counsel. This is the same attorney who assisted Holmes in ripping off Fred Nind and countless others in the A.B.C. Copier sales territory scam. (I told you it can give you a headache!)

The William Green suit claimed that Kate Durkee, Hiram S. Campbell, Thomas and Charles Bryan, and the A.B.C. Copier Co. pretend to own real estate (specifically the murder castle at 63rd and Wallace) in order to convert that property to cash for Holmes, the actual owner. They also claimed that Thomas B. Bryan and his brother, Charles, were hiding other assets of the A.B.C. Copier Co. in the way of corporate stocks or stake in the A.B.C. Copier Co. for the benefit of Holmes.

It seems that before Rogers decided to use the judicial system to recoup any losses from the glycerin fiasco, he had probably decided to take matters into his own hands and enlisted the help of the Cook County Sheriff at the time, James H. Gilbert. Only this time, it didn't appear as though the Sheriff was acting in his official capacity, if you know what I mean. It seems that Henry Rogers may have known the Sheriff personally.

James H. Gilbert was born in 1844 in Toronto of New England parents. He attended the University of Toronto, studied law and was admitted to the bar in 1865. In 1867, he came to Chicago and married Miss Ella K. Huntley in 1870. He was a real estate man and a member of the City Council until 1874, when he retired from real estate and stayed with politics. In 1886, he was elected clerk of the Criminal Court, and in 1890, he was elected as Sheriff on the Republican ticket and served in that capacity until 1894, when he became president of the Garden City Banking and Trust Company, which later became the Metropolitan Trust and Savings Company. I have a feeling that Rogers, being a former banker and real estate person himself, may have known Gilbert socially.

According to a complaint filed by Kate Durkee, on August 22, 1891, William Green, Henry J. Rogers, and James H. Gilbert broke into her apartment building on August 15th. There was no address given in the complaint, but it was more than likely the building at 63rd and Wallace. Durkee claimed that they had broken four doors into pieces and had damaged the locks and hinges of those doors amounting to $200 in damage. She also claimed that the three men stole various items from the building to include an 8 horsepower boiler, a 5 horsepower engine, one lot of bedding and a mixer that came to about $1,000. She believed that they had converted the stolen property to cash for their personal use. She also stated that they created a "great noise and disturbance" for an extended period of time, scaring her and her tenants. She was not able to supply her tenants with steam power, heat and hot water, and was thereby deprived of the ability to charge rent during this period. She was suing for $10,000 (a nice round number that Holmes loved to use in his scams). I am sure that this is the same James H. Gilbert who was Sheriff at the time because the court case included a summons served by the Cook County Coroner, Henry L. Hartz. The Coroner is the only person in the county with arrest powers over the sheriff himself and would not be able to be served by one of his own deputies as was the custom on all other summons services.

The case continued for almost two years without much movement from either side. (Holmes was not known to follow through on any court cases, including that of his divorce from his first wife, Clara Lovering.) On August 4, 1893, Durkee dismissed the case without cost to either party through her attorney, Wharton Plummer.

COULD THE "DEVIL" IN THE WHITE CITY HAVE BRUSHED SHOULDERS WITH THE "CHIEF" IN THE WHITE CITY?

One of the key characters in Erik Larsen's book was the Chief of Construction, Daniel H. Burnham. Burnham had long-standing experience with large construction projects and his knack for bringing together the greatest architects, engineers, and craftsmen made the seemingly impossible task of constructing the fair a successful reality. In 1888, the architectural team of Daniel Burnham and John Root completed the Rookery Building. It still stands in the financial district of Chicago at the southwest corner of Adams and LaSalle. At eleven stories high, the building was one of the grandest of its time. The firm of Burnham and Root moved their offices to the building the same year it opened. In the 1892 Lakeside Directory of Chicago, Daniel Burnham's listing read:

> BURNHAM, DANIEL H. Chief of Bureau of Construction World's Fair, and architect 1143 Rookery Bldg.

The William Green & Co. was running an advertisement in the *Chicago Tribune* at the same time as Burnham was planning the fair and they listed their warehouse at 544-554 North Water Street and their office as "1169 Rookery Building"!

Whether William Green was an alias for Holmes or a shady business partner with the real or alias name of William Green or Francis Green, the fact remains that while Daniel Burnham was busy planning the magnificent splendor of "The White City," he could have ridden the elevator alongside the devil who planned to use the same splendor as his hunting grounds. At the time of the writing of this book, there is a movie adaptation of *The Devil in the White City* in development by Warner Bros. with Leonardo DiCaprio playing the part of H.H. Holmes. I wonder if the producers know how likely it was that Mudgett and Burnham actually came face to face?

FADE TO BLACK

I could find no trace of William or Francis Green following the exit of Holmes from Chicago in early 1894 or of the William Green & Co. The young farm boy, Gerard Riddell, also seemed to drop off the face of the map as well, although he probably never made it out of England alive in 1893. Henry J. Rogers continued out of the 544 North Water warehouse as the Henry J. Rogers & Co. until his death in 1896.

Many people claim that the number of Holmes's victims could range into the hundreds, but the only verifiable deaths are that of Texas sisters Annie and Minnie Williams; Mrs. Julia L. Connor and her daughter, Pearl

The historic Rookery Building, designed by Architects Burnham and Root. Burnham's offices were on the 11th floor, along with the offices of the William Green & Co. for a time. The building still stands at the southeast corner of Adams and LaSalle Streets in Chicago.

The Devil, The White City, William Green, and The Cook County Sheriff

Connor; Miss Emaline C. Cigrand; Robert E. Phelps (possibly Cigrand's fiancé or another alias of Ben Pitezel); Emily Van Tassel; George H. Thomas (an insurance dupe in Mississippi); and Benjamin Pitezel and his children, Alice, Nellie, and Howard Pitezel.

Holmes finally met his fate when he was arrested on November 17, 1894 in Boston where he was held on an outstanding horse theft warrant out of Texas. He was eventually charged with the death of his long-time associate Benjamin Pitezel and hanged on May 7, 1896. He requested that an autopsy not be performed on his body. It is uncertain how much Holmes was influenced by his involvement with the cement and warehousing company known as the William Green & Co. and how many bodies he may have been tempted to dispose of with the aid of the Chicago River and thousands of pounds of cement, but I find it interesting that he also requested that, immediately after his death, his body be completely covered in cement inside his casket and the casket itself be completely covered in cement in the grave. Holmes's requests were granted and he was buried in an unmarked grave at Holy Cross Cemetery in Yeadon, Pennsylvania.

The Post Office at 63rd and Wallace Streets in Chicago that stands approximately on the same site of the Holmes "Murder Castle."

The Haunted Palace of Lincoln Park

The Brewster Apartments, currently a condominium building, is a lesser-known gem in Chicago history and architecture. I really didn't pay much attention to the building until a friend of mine who was studying at DePaul University moved in. I remember his father telling me that his son had found an apartment in a very historic Chicago building. I recognized the name and I had actually seen the building before, although I didn't realize it at the time. In the original MGM Studios movie *Child's Play* (1988), the main building where "Chucky" the killer doll lived was in the Brewster Apartments. The building is featured pretty heavily in the movie and there is a scene where a woman is thrown out of a window and falls to her death that really creeped me out after I had done the research on the building. The reason that I decided to include the building in this book is not only because of its historic significance, but also due to its strange beginnings, which I wouldn't even be aware of if it wasn't for my first extraordinary visit to the building.

I am a big fan of history and Chicago architecture, so when my friend was describing the building to me with its original operator-run elevator and lighted walkways, I just had to see it for myself. I visited the building with my camera in hand to capture some of the beauty and nostalgia that my friend had described to me. I wasn't disappointed. The building was amazing! I felt as though I was being transported back in time to the

"The Lincoln Park Palace," now known as the Brewster Apartments, still stands at 500 W. Diversey Parkway with the "Ladies Entrance" at 2800 North Pine Grove Avenue.

later 1800s when the building was first built. The elevator operator was not on duty, though, which was rather disappointing. I really wanted to ride in one of the only remaining elevators of its kind in Chicago.

The building has a very open feel to it and I stood in the lobby and looked up to the atrium and the large skylights above. The original iron staircases and lighted glass walkways were amazing. I had heard that Charlie Chaplin supposedly occupied the penthouse, which is really the seventh floor of the building, but I have not been able to verify that with any research or reliable sources as of yet. Still, I wanted to see it. As I was standing across from the seventh-floor apartment, I had this overwhelming feeling of anxiety, dread, and nausea. I do not consider myself a "sensitive" person as some refer to themselves, but I had this horrible feeling of falling! Granted, you can look down through the open atrium all the way to the lobby floor, and I've had a similar feeling when I have been up in the Sears (now Willis) Tower, but really nothing this strong before. I remember feeling silly when I told my friend, "Something terrible happened here." I felt a little like that small psychic woman from the movie *Poltergeist*. I asked my friend if he had heard anything about the place having a history or being haunted and he said that he had heard a few things from neighbors, but didn't want to hear details because he had to live there. I knew at this point that I had to research the building.

A LONG WAY DOWN

In 1892, Bjoerne Edwards, publisher of the trade paper, *American Contractor*, at 108 Randolph Street, began construction on a lifelong dream of building the finest apartment house in the world, although the cornerstone wasn't laid until July 14, 1894. The *American Contractor* is historically significant in its own right because it published information on pending Chicago construction projects and issuances of building permits. There is actually an online index to the published permits from 1898-1912 on the Chicago History Museum's website. Mr. Edwards was from Norway and came to America as a boy. He worked on a farm in Wisconsin as a youth and afterward came to Chicago to do manual labor until he had enough money to go to school. He attended the theological seminaries of the Lutheran Church in Iowa and Illinois.

The building was to be named the Lincoln Park Palace and was designed by architect Enock Hill Turnock who came to America from England at the age of 14. The Turnock family settled in Elkhart, Indiana, but Enock was educated, at least in part, at the Art Institute of Chicago, and for nine years was with architect W.L.B. Jenney. Turnock had his individual office in Chicago until 1907 when he returned to Elkhart, Indiana, where he designed many residences, including the Ruthmere Mansion (1910) and public buildings, such as the Elkhart City Hall.

The building is made up almost entirely of pink jasper and both entrances are made of beautiful polished jasper granite. The interior courtyard construction is of iron and prismatic lights and the interior wood finishing was originally of mahogany, oak, and red birch. The east entrance on Pine Grove was known as "the ladies entrance." It was amazingly modern at the time of its construction, with both gas and electric lights and telephones in all of the rooms that connected each to the office. The ground floor had office, restaurant, drug store, physician, and messenger space. The room that opens to the rotunda was actually first used as a ladies' waiting room and a sitting room for gentlemen.

Bjoerne Edwards' neighbors in the upscale area were not thrilled about him building a large apartment building on the northwest corner of Diversey and Park (Park is now Pine Grove Avenue) and were vocal about their opposition. Some neighbors said that Edward was acting in a "queer way" ever since the building started and said that it was obvious evidence of a "disturbed mind." There were also a number of obstacles to the construction, such as the strike of the quarrymen. Edwards had leased a quarry in Jasper, Minnesota, from where all the stone for the building came, and the union workers objected to Edwards' use of non-union labor. Edwards did not give in to the union workers' demand to fire the non-union workers, so the project was put on hold until Edwards could replace the striking union workers.

View of the floor directly below the penthouse floor of the Brewster Apartments.

On July 31, 1895, Edward's wife, Mary C.C. Edwards, was away in Oshkosh, Wisconsin, tending to the funeral of her mother. Mr. Edwards was on the roof of the unfinished building directing workmen regarding some fireproofing issue. As he approached the ladder to descend, he stepped on a poorly secured scaffolding board and fell eight stories through the courtyard to the lobby below. He was picked up unconscious and taken to Alexian Brother's Hospital where he died two hours later.

When I read the account of the death of Edwards in an August 16, 1896 edition of the *Chicago Daily Tribune*, the hairs on my neck really did stand on end. I had been standing literally no more than twenty feet from where Edwards had fallen to his death when I had that overwhelming feeling of dread a short time earlier! Maybe there is something to the theory that energy can be left behind by someone who has died suddenly due to some tragic event.

Just three months earlier, Edwards had secured a loan of $70,000 to complete construction of the building and at the time of his death there was enough left to ensure that the building would be completed.

Following Edwards' death, his wife, Mary, finished the project in September of 1896, at a final cost of $300,000. She purchased the building adjacent to and west of the palace, which is today the YAK-ZIES on Diversey bar at 506 W. Diversey. The Lincoln Park Palace, however, never made a profit and a General Henry Strong of Lake Geneva, Wisconsin, brought suit against Mary, as a $20,000 stakeholder in the property. He took possession of the property in January of 1901. As late as 1900, Mary Edwards was living at the Lincoln Park Palace as a renter with her sister, Frieda Daib. Her brother, Frederick Daib, and his wife, Mathilda, and daughter, Agnes, lived and rented at the Lincoln Park Palace as well.

Some other residents of the building had met their fate as a result of tragedies, too.

William H. Collins, a traveling salesman for the retail store of Wanamaker & Brown (absorbed by Macy's in 1995), was in his buggy along Lake Shore Drive and Bellevue shortly before the 4th of July in 1899, when a firecracker exploded, frightening his horse. The horse

View from the lobby looking straight up to the skylight, which is the height from which Bjoerne Edwards would have fallen.

ran off with the buggy and Collins jumped from it and was killed upon hitting the ground. His funeral was held at his residence at the Brewster and he was buried at Rosehill Cemetery.

Another tragic tale of a resident of the Brewster Apartments is the one of Mrs. Mary Raymond-Greiner. She was Miss Mary Raymond before her marriage to Mr. Shelden S. Greiner, a Chicago salesman for the Stewart Manufacturing Company, in April of 1924. Mr. Greiner suffered a fatal stroke the day after the marriage and died within four days. She had also lost her father and sister within the prior four years, and with the death of her new husband, she was left with very little family. In July of 1924, about three months after the death of her husband, she was aboard the lake steamer *North American,* which left Buffalo, New York on Saturday, July 19th, and arrived in Chicago on Tuesday, July 22nd. Miss Raymond-Greiner never got off the boat in Chicago. Other passengers on the steamer remember seeing her up on deck on Saturday evening, but not a soul remembers seeing her after that. Raymond-Greiner's attorney, Harry A. White, sent a message to Detroit detectives on the odd chance that she disembarked there when it was docked in Detroit for thirty minutes on Sunday. The detectives could find no trace of her. The attorney also contacted relatives in Elgin, Illinois, but they had not heard from her either. The management of the steamer line told her attorney that the only articles missing from her belongings were a nightdress, her wedding ring, and a wristwatch. Her attorney and family had come to grips with the fact that, due to her depressed condition and the circumstances, she took her own life by leaping from the deck of the *North American* into the waters of Lake Erie.

I know that something still exists at the Brewster Apartments. Whether it is the spirit of Bjoerne Edwards who fell to his death in the building he almost completed, the spirit of William H. Collins who was killed by the actions of a runaway horse, or the pitiful spirit of 42-year-old Mary Raymond-Greiner, who took her own life after losing her husband of only one day. For all we know, it could be all three or more, but even if you don't believe in hauntings, you owe it to yourself to visit this very beautiful historic Chicago landmark.

A view of the lobby of the Brewster Apartments.

Chicago and
the R.M.S. *Titanic*

In addition to the 1893 World's Columbian Exposition, I, like so many others, have found a particular fascination with the events surrounding the now legendary R.M.S. *Titanic*. I had written an online article about the Hippach family being one of the families with the worst luck in Chicago. A woman by the name of Denise Vanaria had contacted me because she worked at the *Titanic* museum, "*Titanic*, the Experience," in Orlando, Florida, and she played the part of Ida Hippach, one of the first-class passengers. Denise is an amazing *Titanic* historian and travels around the world doing first-person plays as Mrs. Thomas Andrews, the wife of the *Titanic's* chief designer. I also had found out that when she performs as Ida Hippach in Florida, or Mrs. Thomas Andrews on the road, she always dresses in authentic Edwardian Era dresses. In fact, she has the largest private collection of such dresses in the nation and she restores them all by hand! As fate would have it, another friend of mine, Bruce Beveridge, who I met when working on my last book, when dealing with the legend of Resurrection Mary, is one of the world's foremost authorities on the RMS *Titanic's* engineering and construction and has authored and

**Tongue-in-cheek author's rendition of the
R.M.S.** *Titanic* **leaving Chicago.**

The R.M.S. *Titanic***, May 31, 1911, approximately one year before
its fateful maiden voyage.** *Library of Congress, Prints & Photographs
Division [reproduction number, LC-USZ62-56585].*

co-authored a great many books on the subject to include what many consider to be the most comprehensive work to date, *Titanic: The Ship Magnificent* (2008, The History Press). I found out that Denise and Bruce go back quite a ways. I was floored when she actually invited me to speak at her Chicago area presentations on the *Titanic* and its Chicago links culminating with the 100th Anniversary Presentation at the Joliet, Illinois Public Library. (A resident of Joliet, Miss Helmina Josefina Nillson, was a survivor on lifeboat #13.) Denise is unbelievably emotional about the *Titanic* and actually becomes Mrs. Thomas Andrews during her performances and had brought me to tears more than once. Her father, Stanley Kuta, was her greatest supporter and curator of the many artifacts that have been donated to her over the years and she dedicates all of her performances to him. If you ever get a chance to see one of her performances, do so!

PREMONITIONS

There were many myths, legends, and coincidences surrounding the sinking of the *Titanic*. There seemed to be many so-called premonitions of various forms predicting the disaster and one in particular almost defies coincidence.

As with many other major disasters, there seems to be an air of "We knew this would happen" after the tragedy takes place. I think all of us have had some apprehension when boarding a plane, or a boat, or an amusement park ride, for that matter. Maybe that is part of the fun and excitement of travel itself. However, for some, it is more than simple apprehension. We have all heard stories of people who, for some reason, at the last minute, cancelled plans, and by some luck or divine intervention seemingly succeeded in cheating death. Did the same situation occur for some of those who avoided or boarded the *Titanic*?

One of the most famous examples of a fateful premonition had nothing to do with any of the individual passengers, but involves author Morgan Robertson. Robertson wrote a book called *Futility*. The subject of the book had to do with the largest steamship ever built called the "*Titan*." The story centers around the main character of the book, John Rowland, a former military officer who battles with alcoholism and must eventually take a position as deckhand on the ship. There are eerie similarities between the fictional *Titan* and the

Titanic. In the book, the *Titan* was "the largest craft afloat and the greatest of the works of men (800 feet, displacing 75,000 tons) and was considered unsinkable. The *Titanic* was 882 feet and displacing 63,000 tons. Both the *Titanic* and the *Titan* suffered from a shortage of lifeboats. Both ships had a passenger capacity of 3,000. Both ships were traveling in the North Atlantic; however, the *Titan* was going from the U.S. to England, not vice versa. Both ships struck an iceberg on their starboard side in the month of April, 400 miles from Newfoundland.

All of these similarities and yet Robertson published his book in 1898, roughly fourteen years before the *Titanic* disaster and nine years before the first planning meeting was ever held to discuss the possibility of the *Titanic* and their sister ships in 1907.

Not everything was spot on, however. Of the *Titan's* 2,200 passengers, only 13 survived. Of the *Titanic's* 2,223 passengers, 706 survived and 1,517 were lost. The actual *Titanic* split in half and sank; the *Titan* capsized and went down bow first.

TEMPTING FATE

Sailors are probably one of the most superstitious bunches that anyone may have the pleasure of meeting, and rightfully so, in my opinion. For anyone who has boarded a boat of any considerable size and been tossed around, seemingly effortlessly, by a large body of water knows that you would like to have as much luck on your side as possible.

Some instances of tempting fate attributed to the *Titanic* disaster are:

The Name of the *Titanic* itself

The name "Titanic" itself was looked upon as a direct insult to the Greek God Poseidon who ruled over all waters of the Earth. The Titans were a giant race of Gods who were at war with the Greek Gods of Olympus. The Greek Gods eventually won out and Poseidon, when angered, would slam his trident into the ground causing earthquakes, stormy seas, and shipwrecks. To name a ship after the enemies of Poseidon was to some egotistical in the least and deadly at its worst. Today, it would be the equivalent of going to church wearing a shirt that said "Satan Rules."

There is the belief that one of the *Titanic's* sister ships, the *Britannic*, was at some point in time supposed to be named the "*Gigantic*." There were several newspaper reports and Harland and Wolff's anchor supplier referred to the third ship in the Olympic Class as the "*Gigantic*," but the name did not stick. However, the fate of the ships seem to echo the greek mythology in that both the *Titanic* and "*Gigantic*" sank (the *Britannic* in WWI) and only the *Olympic* survived to be scrapped in 1935.

As early as June 1, 1911, almost a year before the *Titanic* disaster, the editor of the *Belfast Morning News* and *Irish News* questioned the choice of names when he stated that Zeus "...smote the strong and daring Titans with thunderbolts; and their final abiding place was in some limbo beneath the lowest depths of Tartarus."

The Titanic's Extravagance

Many believed, including many first-class passengers, that the sheer opulence and extravagance of the first-class amenities was a prideful and egotistical display that would be frowned upon by a higher power.

In fact, first-class passenger and survivor, Colonel Archibald Gracie, stated:

> The pleasure and comfort which all of us enjoyed upon this floating palace, with its extraordinary provisions for such purposes, seemed an ominous feature to many of us, including myself, who felt it almost too good to last without some terrible retribution inflicted by the hand of an angry omnipotence. Our sentiment in this respect was voiced by one of the most able and distinguished of our fellow passengers, Mr. Charles Hays, President of the Canadian Grand Trunk Railroad...The White Star, the Cunard, and the Hamburg-American Lines are now devoting their attention to a struggle for supremacy in obtaining the most luxurious appointments for their ships, but the time will soon come when the greatest and most appalling of all disasters at sea will be the result.

Hays was body 307.

The Titanic was Never Christened

There are records going back as far as 3,000 B.C. of seafaring ships being launched with ceremony, prayers, and sacrifices to the gods to help ensure the safety of the ship and crew during a ship's useful lifetime. These later were referred to as "christenings" in the

Christian-based civilizations and usually involved the pouring of wine or the breaking of a bottle across the bow or stern of the ship. Again, the superstitious sailors believed that ships, similarly to humans, had souls and therefore were in need of a baptism or christening, to ensure the blessings of God on the ship and crew.

Harland and Wolff, the builders of the *Titanic*, did not christen any of the ships they built. As one shipworker said at the time, "We just builds 'er and shoves 'er in."

The Titanic was Generally Believed to be Unsinkable

So many people believed, or at least said publicly, that the ship was "unsinkable," that it was what I call a blatant violation and taunting of Murphy and his law. While the exact origins of the contemporary version and naming of Murphy's Law is in dispute, I personally believe that the U.S. version of it stems from the World's Columbian Exposition and was coined by the Exposition's Fire Chief on July 10, 1893.

Bruce Ismay, the much-despised managing director of the White Star Line, said at the British enquiry:

> I think the position was taken up that the ship was looked upon as practically unsinkable; she was looked upon as being a lifeboat in herself.

Much of this belief stemmed from the fact that the *Titanic* was designed with sixteen watertight compartments and designed to float with any two flooded or all three forward compartments flooded.

The highly respected trade journal of the time, *Shipbuilder*, had published regarding the Olympic Class liners:

> so that in the event of accident, or at any time when it may be considered advisable, the captain can, by simply moving an electric switch, instantly close the doors throughout and make the vessel practically unsinkable.

Titanic survivor, Elmer Taylor, stated that he heard Captain Smith explaining that the ship could be "cut crosswise into three pieces and each piece would float."

Captain Smith was quoted in an article in 1907 in the *New York Times* about modern shipbuilding in general after the maiden voyage of the *Adriatic:*

Capt. Smith maintained that shipbuilding was such a perfect art nowadays that absolute disaster, involving the passengers on a great modern liner, was quite unthinkable. Whatever happened, he contended, there would be time before the vessel sank to save the lives of every person on board. "I will go a bit further," he said. " I will say that I cannot imagine any condition which would cause a ship to founder. I cannot conceive of any vital disaster happening to this vessel. Modern shipbuilding has gone beyond that."

On April 15, 1912, as reports of the disaster were first coming in, Philip Franklin, Vice President of the White Star Line, stated:

We place absolute confidence in the *Titanic*. We believe that the boat is unsinkable.

The only problem was that as Franklin's words were being spoken, the *Titanic* already lay 12,460 feet below the surface of the North Atlantic.

The Hull Number of the Titanic was a Deliberate Attempt to Sabotage the Liner

There have been quite a few stories about the supposed hull number of the *Titanic* being a deliberate anti-Catholic statement. Rumors circulated about the hull number of the boat being 3909 04, which, when viewed in a mirror, would have appeared similar to the letters, "No Pope."

While it was true that tensions were high between Catholics and Protestants and that the Harland and Wolff shipyards were in a Protestant area of Belfast, Lord Pirrie would more than likely not tolerate any tensions that would have jeopardized the successful building of his ships. In fact, jobs at Harland and Wolff were prized among both Catholics and Protestants and Pirrie hired competent employees regardless of their religious beliefs.

It is also a fact that the *Titanic* was never assigned a hull number of 3909 04, but a build or hull number of 401 and a Board of Trade number of 131,428.

THE HIPPACHS—QUITE POSSIBLY CHICAGO'S UNLUCKIEST FAMILY

I don't know if you, as a reader, are old enough to remember a character from *The Flintstones* cartoon named Schleprock. He made several appearances in the cartoon show, but was known for bringing bad luck with him wherever he went, and sometimes, the characters around him were victimized for just being in his presence. The Hippach Family of Chicago may just be our version of Schleprock.

I first became aware of the Hippach family on a research visit to Rosehill Cemetery, one of the city's oldest and prettiest. I was speaking to a longtime employee of the cemetery and he mentioned the Hippach family to me. I was originally there to take photos of the monuments of some of Chicago's more well-known residents, such as John G. Shedd, Richard Warren Sears, Mayor John "Long John" Wentworth, and others.

Ida Sophia Hippach was born Ida Sophia Fisher on November 24, 1866, in Chicago and later married Louis A. Hippach, who was the co-owner of Tyler and Hippach Co., a plate glass dealer in Chicago. The Hippachs had four children: Robert L., born November 1889; Archibald A., born September 1892; Gertrude B. (Jean), born October 1894; and Howard H., born May 1896.

Louis A. Hippach, co-founder of the Tyler-Hippach Glass Company.
Photograph courtesy of The Hippach Family.

The beginning of the family's struggle with fate started, as best I could determine, with the loss of both young sons, (Robert, who would have been 14 at the time, and Archie, who would have been 12) in the infamous Chicago Iroquois Theatre fire of 1903. For those readers not familiar with the great fire, it occurred on December 30, 1903, at a matinee performance of the play, *Mr. Bluebeard*. The crowd consisted of mainly women and children and numbered at about 1,000. Over 600 innocents died in that fire and the political repercussions that followed the enormous loss of life formed the basis for many of the theatre fire safety codes in use today by not only the city of Chicago, but the nation.

There have also been numerous ghost stories associated with the alleyway behind the current Ford Center for the Performing Arts that occupies the same location as the ill-fated Iroquois. A large number of individuals lost their lives in that alleyway when they fell attempting to crawl across ladders that had been stretched from the windows of the then Northwestern Dental School to the blocked fire escape of the upper level of the theatre. I have been in that alleyway and there is a feeling of sadness or foreboding that I have felt even during broad daylight.

Ida Hippach had a very hard time adjusting to the death of her two sons and decided to take a European vacation with her daughter, Jean, to attempt to relax and calm her nerves. On the 10th of April 1912, while in Cherbourg, France, Mrs. Hippach decided to purchase tickets for her and her daughter on a luxury liner bound for New York City. They were told that they purchased the last two remaining first-class tickets for this maiden voyage of the liner and they felt lucky to have been able to purchase them. At almost midnight on the 14th of April 1912, Mrs. Hippach and her daughter were asleep when the luxury liner struck an iceberg! Yes, you guessed it; the two had "luckily" booked a trip on the RMS *Titanic*!

Titanic **survivor Jean Hippach, 1913, the year after the** *Titanic* **disaster, when she would have been about 18 years old.** *Photograph courtesy of The Hippach Family.*

They, however, were two of the fortunate 711 survivors of the disaster and picked up by the *Carpathia* after rowing about two miles to get to the rescue ship. The *Carpathia* headed to New York and Mr. Hippach and their remaining son, Howard, traveled to New York to meet them. They all arrived safely back in Chicago on April 21, 1912, aboard the train, the *Twentieth Century Limited*.

If the Iroquois Theatre fire and the sinking of the *Titanic* were not enough, on October 29, 1914, Howard Hippach, their only remaining son, died in a vehicle crash in Lake Genevea, Wisconsin, at the age of 19.

Less than one year later, Jean, the only remaining child was a passenger in a vehicle driven by Hugo Carlson. On August 29, 1914, Hugo and Jean were driving along Lake Shore Drive and were just north of Fullerton Avenue when their vehicle struck and killed an 8-year-old boy named John Dredling while his father, mother, and four siblings watched. Carlson jumped from the vehicle to render aid to the boy and while he and Jean were outside the vehicle trying to help the little boy and console his family, an unknown passerby stole a briefcase from their automobile!

Things seemed to be looking up for the Hippach's when Louis and Ida announced the wedding of their daughter, Jean, to Kahalmar Unander-Scharin, a graduate of the Stockholm University, a reserve officer in the Royal Eight Dragoons, and son to late Consul Egil Unander-Scharin. They were married on January 3, 1920, in Chicago, and moved to 930 Central Park in New York City. They had three children, Howard, Jean, and Louise, but then Jean's luck didn't hold. On November 18, 1929, her husband was on board the *Twentieth Century Limited*, the same train that brought Jean and her mother back from New York after the *Titanic* tragedy. The *Twentieth Century Limited* has its own history that is beyond the scope of this book, but was known as the "Train of Tycoons and Stars" and ran nightly between New York and Chicago. Mr. Unander-Scharin was en route to New York from Chicago, and according to Jean's account, he committed adultery with a woman while participating in a "pajama party" aboard the train. She filed for divorce, which was granted on June 2, 1930. She returned to the Chicago area with her children.

In addition to the aforementioned tragedies, Mr. Louis A. Hippach's glass company, Tyler and Hippach, was bombed by radical labor groups in 1922, and an employee, George Linton, was robbed at gunpoint by three assailants making off with $5,000 in company payroll in 1926.

Eventually, it seemed that fate had mercy on the Hippachs when Louis A. passed away on May 30, 1935, and his wife, Ida, followed suit on September 22, 1940, both dying of seemingly non-violent causes.

It appeared that Jean tried once more for marital bliss when she married a doctor and reserve medical officer, Dr. Budd Clarke Corbus, Jr. of Evanston. Jean was living in Lake Forest, Illinois, at the time and they had a very private ceremony at her home on January 26, 1942. Unfortunately, the attempt failed miserably and they were together only five days when, according to her second divorce proceedings, Dr. Corbus abandoned her. The divorce was final almost one year later.

Khalmar Unander-Scharin, Jean Hippach's first husband. *Photograph courtesy of The Hippach Family.*

The Unander-Scharin children from left to right: Harold H., Louise, and Jean. *Photograph courtesy of The Hippach Family.*

I had the wonderful opportunity to speak with a grandson of Jean Hippach who shared with me recollections of his grandmother. He said that she was a very proper woman, although they always referred to her as "Geyegee" as sort of a nickname. He believed it came about when one of the other grandkids could not pronounce her name correctly and it just kind of "stuck."

With regard to the *Titanic*, he always thought it was strange that when she spoke of the events of that fateful night, she always recalled it as though it was "no big deal." He remembered that she told him that she had just started to fall asleep when she felt the vibrations of the ship. A man came into their cabin and told them to put on their life vests and come out on deck. She remembered putting on their fur coats over their night dresses and going out on deck. Once on deck things were pretty confusing, and at one point, a woman came out on deck completely naked and appeared as though she'd had too much to drink. She jumped overboard and probably did not make it, since it was about a ten-story drop from the deck to the water, let alone the freezing temperatures of the North Atlantic. One of the last lifeboats was already being lowered and it was John Jacob Astor himself who guided her and her mother, Ida, to a porthole on one of the lower decks in time to squeeze through the porthole and into the already lowering boat. Astor had actually given his grandmother Jean his flask, but it had somehow disappeared within the family.

Jean Hippach, in 1919, the year before her marriage to Khalmar Unander-Scharin.
Photograph courtesy of The Hippach Family.

Two things stuck out in Jean's memory of the disaster and one of them was the unbelievable size of the iceberg. The other was the shouting. She remembered as the ship sank, it broke into two, and then seemed to come back together as it was going down. After the ship was gone, she remembered hearing for hours the voices of women shouting the names of their husbands from the lifeboats in the hopes that they would answer back. This went on for hours with no answers until they gradually faded away as the women came to realize they wouldn't hear back from their husbands.

He always thought it was curious that after the *Titanic*, his grandmother went on many other cruises and was never afraid to board a ship (she may have thought that the worst possible thing that could happen already happened, so she must be safe). She, however, was terrified to fly and would never get on a plane. One time when he was flying as a child, he asked her to help him get on his flight, just to see if she would step aboard a plane, and while she helped him get settled on the plane, she literally almost passed out being on the inside of the plane, even though she knew she wouldn't be traveling on it!

He remembers that Jean loved dogs and would take in any and every stray that she came across and that she was also a terrible driver. He remembered the grandkids being terrified in the back seat when "Geyegee" would be driving with a number of dogs in the front seat and trying to control them while not watching the road!

On November 14, 1974, Jean Hippach Scharin passed away quietly in her home, 796 Seaview Avenue, Wianno, Massachusetts, at the age of 79, leaving her three children and nine grandchildren.

So the next time you think that you are having a bad day or that things don't seem to be going your way, take a moment to reflect on the Hippachs, and if you find yourself paying your respects to one of Chicago's unluckiest families at Rosehill Cemetery, be sure to look both ways before crossing the street!

William T. Stead

A Spiritualist Aboard The *Titanic*

Mr. Stead was born in England on July 5, 1849, to a local minister. In the 1880s, he was the editor of the *Pall Mall Gazette*, a Liberal daily. He was actually very much a reformer and crusader against many social injustices of his time. He published an article entitled, "The Maiden Tribute of Modern Babylon" in which he stated that for the sum of £5 he could hire the services of a 13-year-old prostitute. He was jailed for a time in England due to his outspoken views on the tolerance that the British officials had concerning the "white slave trade." There was such a public outcry that the government was compelled to release him. He later went on to publish his own monthly journal, *Review of Reviews*, and it soon became one of the most influential publications of its time.

Stead spent a good amount of time in Chicago between 1893 and 1894 during the World's Columbian Exposition and prided himself with getting to know the "real" Chicago, the part of Chicago that it did not want to share with the rest of the world during the publicity of "The World's Fair." He wanted to learn about the seedier side of Chicago and expose the workings of its brothels, saloons, and pawn shops. He would typically disguise himself as a person from the lower rung of society and wander the levee districts meeting people, looking for work, and sharing the stories of the less fortunate. His energy level was unequaled when it came to social reform and Jane Addams herself would welcome Stead into the main building of Hull House (currently a museum run by the University of Illinois at Chicago) late at night when he was exhausted after a hard day's work and he would enjoy sitting by the warming fire and tell her stories of his escapades. He wrote of these Chicago experiences in a publication entitled, *If Christ Came to Chicago*. According to some accounts, this publication gained him more notoriety than any of his previous works. It did not paint the City of Chicago in a very positive light and he didn't make any fast friends with the residents. By Stead's account in the preface of the British Edition, over 70,000 copies were ordered before the first book came off the press in Chicago. He stated that people would just

William T. Stead. *Library of Congress, Prints & Photographs Division [reproduction number: LC-DIG-ggbain-03860].*

have to wait because he refused to use anything but union labor to produce the book. The name W.T. Stead would be linked to the City of Chicago from that point forward.

Stead was also a steadfast believer in the rapidly growing spiritualist movement of the late 19th and early 20th centuries. In 1893, Stead published a spiritualist journal called *Borderland*. Here is where his other link to the City of Chicago lies. A Chicago woman by the name of Julia Ames visited Stead in England in the late 1800s and the two became quick friends. Julia was an editor at the *Union Signal of Chicago,* which was a literary arm of the Women's Christian Temperance Union. Julia died shortly after their meeting and Stead claimed to be communicating with her using "automatic writing." He would place a writing instrument in his hand and various deceased persons, including Julia, would communicate with him by compelling his hand to scribe their messages. "Julia" had even gone so far as saying that while people were grieving their loved ones, their loved ones were desperately attempting to contact them in order to console them. Stead continued communication with Julia for many years after and even created a group of spiritualist friends known as "Julia's Bureau," which met regularly to conduct séances.

Stead had predicted that he would die from either lynching or drowning. A clairvoyant friend of his told him that he would be kicked to death in the streets of London, which was probably more of an educated guess, given the fact that Stead liked to "stir the pot," so to speak.

Stead had written at least two prior articles that could be considered by some to be an uncanny prediction of his fate. In 1886, he published an article entitled "How the Mail Steamer Went Down in the Mid-Atlantic, by a Survivor." The story was about a ship that collided with another ship and the main reason for the extraordinary loss of lives being a shortage of lifeboats. It was said that he also made the statement that this could actually happen if ships were continually allowed to sail with an inadequate supply of lifeboats. (The *Titanic* sailed with only twenty, which would have covered barely half the passengers if each lifeboat was filled to capacity.) In 1892, he published a story, "From the Old World to the New," about a Mr. Compton who was traveling on the White Star ship *Majestic*. The *Majestic* was a real ship in the White Star line, but the story was fiction. In the story, there were two psychics aboard who received telepathic messages from survivors of a shipwreck just ahead of the *Majestic*. It seemed that their ship had collided with an iceberg and the survivors were huddled together atop the iceberg waiting to be rescued. Mr. Compton seemed to be very similar to Stead himself, in that Compton used "automatic writing" to communicate with the survivors of the shipwreck and convinced the Captain of the ship to change course and pick up the stranded survivors based on his psychic communication. In an eerie coincidence, three years after the publishing of the story, the real *Majestic* received a new captain none other than Captain E.J. Smith who went down with the *Titanic*!

Many of Stead's spiritualist friends begged Stead not to board the *Titanic* and many thought he was tempting fate because of the stories that he had written. They also worried that he wore a crucifix bearing a skull and crossbones that was thought to have belonged to Catherine the Great and to bring bad luck to all who possessed it.

In maybe one of Stead's final acts of supernatural defiance he delighted in telling the story of a cursed mummy while conversing with other passengers on the evening of Friday, April 12th. In the story, Stead describes a mysterious message that is etched on the mummy's case and that whoever reads the inscription out loud would suffer a violent death. Stead then promptly reads the message out loud and lets the other passengers know that the telling of his tale had taken them all past midnight, which meant it was now the 13th of the month. This story eventually took on a life of its own after the sinking of the *Titanic* and rumors were floating around (no pun intended) that the mummy was actually within the *Titanic's* cargo holds and that it was somehow recovered and shipped back to the states where it found its way onto the RMS *Lusitania* when it left New York on May 1, 1915, bound for Liverpool. On May 7th, about eleven miles off the southern coast of Ireland, the *Lusitania* was torpedoed by a German U-boat. The ship sank in eighteen minutes and took with it 1,198 souls. It makes for a good story, but Stead had actually concocted this whole tale with one of his friends.

In the moments before the sinking of the *Titanic*, it was said by survivors that Stead could be seen sitting in a leather chair quietly reading, while those on deck were frantically filling lifeboats. It is somewhat ironic that one of the social issues that Stead was very verbal about was the fact that ships were not required to be equipped with adequate lifeboats to insure that all passengers had a seat on one.

Mr. Stead's body was never recovered, but one account of his last moments by Phillip Mock (a survivor) was this:

> Many men were hanging on to rafts in the sea. William T. Stead, the author, and Col. John Jacob Astor clung to a raft. Their feet became frozen and they were compelled to release their hold. Both were drowned.

Befitting a spiritualist, William Stead may not have departed this world completely after the sinking of the great ship. An article appeared in the *Chicago Tribune* on December 7, 1913, and quotes a good friend of Stead's, Major General Sir Alfred Edward Turner. Major General Turner was a career military man who was a Knight Commander in the The Most Honourable Order of the Bath, a British order of chivalry. He was also the military private secretary to Earl Spencer, the Viceroy of Ireland. Major General Turner was also an avid spiritualist researcher.

Turner was quoted in the article:

> "I have been asked to give my recent experiences with reference to communications with W.T. Stead. Within a few days of the wreck of the *Titanic* he appeared to a circle of friends, all psychics, in my house. When I say appeared, I mean that his voice, the well-known voice, was distinctly heard. It grew stronger and stronger, till at last we were conversing with him as if he had been present in earthly shape. We all had known him well and his strong voice could not have been mistaken.
>
> He began by telling us how glad he was to be with us again. He spoke at some length to a lady who had been his private secretary for some years and who had been his able helper. Then he told me about the last moments of the *Titanic* and what took place afterward, when the crowds of disembodied spirits were wandering about as though groping in the dark, having no idea that they had shuffled off their mortal coil and had become denizens of another plane.
>
> Stead set himself at once to help and enlighten them, and countless spirits—in most cases no doubt the dear ones of the victims—appeared to succor them and help them onward and upward.

"Not Milay"

Francis "Frank" Davis Millet was by all accounts an extraordinary man. During his lifetime he was an avid traveler, journalist, author, war correspondent, and painter who spoke and wrote in a half dozen languages. According to an article in the *Chicago Tribune* (November 27, 1892), Millet's ancestors had come to America aboard the *Mayflower* and his home was situated on the land that was purchased from the Native Americans by Miles Standish. He was born November 3, 1846 in Mattapoisett, Massachusetts, and due in large part to his adventurous nature, he enlisted as a drummer boy at 15 years of age with a Massachusetts regiment at the beginning of the Civil War. He was soon promoted to assistant surgeon and assisted his father, a surgeon, during the war effort. It was said that he gained an appreciation for the vivid blood red color that he frequently used in his earlier paintings as a result of his assistant surgeon duties during the war.

He graduated from Harvard University with a Master of Arts degree in 1869 and worked as a reporter for the *Boston Courier* and as a correspondent for the *Advertiser* at the Philadelphia Centennial Exposition.

In the 1870s, he had studios in Rome and in Venice. In 1876, he returned to Boston to assist in painting murals at Trinity Church in Boston. He later studied art at the Royal Academy of Fine Arts in Antwerp, Belgium, where he won silver and gold medals for his work.

He was good friends with Augustus Saint-Gaudens who sculpted both the "Standing Lincoln" in Chicago's Lincoln Park and the statue of the seated Lincoln in Chicago's Grant Park. He was also good friends with writer Mark Twain who was his best man at his 1879 marriage to Elizabeth Merrill in Paris, France.

His link to Chicago started in the summer of 1891, when he originally came to Chicago and was an instructor at the Art Institute. Construction of the World's Columbian Exposition in Chicago was well underway, and sometime between May and November of 1892, Millet replaced William Pretyman as Director of Decoration for the Fair. It was actually Millet who decided on the predominantly white color of the buildings, which ultimately gave the Exposition its nickname "The White City." He decided on a paint consisting of oil and white lead, and due to time constraints, came up with the idea of applying the paint using a hose and special nozzle as opposed to a brush. He was credited with inventing the process of "spray painting." In addition to overseeing the decoration of the Columbian Exposition, he also supplied his own artwork. One of his paintings adorned the vaulted ceiling of the banqueting hall of the New York State Building.

It was known that Millet favored the English pronunciation of his last name and a *Chicago Tribune* article stated:

> It ought to be settled that Mr. Millet is of English extraction, so that people who insist on going about the grounds inquiring for Mr. Millay will quit it and give him the benefit of the English pronunciation, Millet, with an italic breathing on the first syllable.

After the World's Fair in Chicago, he was asked by the War Department to design the Civil War Campaign Medal for both the Army and Navy in 1907. He also became involved in the American Academy in Rome and served as secretary from 1904 to 1911.

In early 1912, Mr. Millet took a trip to Rome for Academy business and took with him his good friend, Major Archibald Willingham Butt. Major Butt (remember we are all adults here) was the military aide to Presidents Taft and Theodore Roosevelt and had just taken six weeks leave from the White House because the constant personal battles between Taft and Roosevelt were starting to take a toll on his health.

On April 10, 1912, Mr. Millet, with ticket number 13509, boarded the RMS *Titanic* at Cherbourg, Normandy, France en route to New York for Academy business. He was joined on the *Titanic* by his good friend Major Butt, who was on his way back to Washington, D.C.

On April 13, 1912, during his last trip to Europe, Daniel Burnham, who appointed Millet as Director of Decorations of the Fair in 1893, boarded the *Titanic's* sister ship, the RMS *Olympic*. The two ships were supposed to pass very close to each other out at sea, but when Burnham attempted to send a message of greeting to Millet on the evening of the 14th via the wireless operator, he was told by the steward that his message was refused by the wireless operator because the *Titanic* had been involved in an accident. Burnham would never see his friend Millet again and would die himself in June of that year.

Some reports of survivors seem to indicate that the last acts of Millet and Butt before the last lifeboats were boarded were to give their life preservers to the last women to leave the ship.

Mr. Millet's body was recovered from the frigid waters of the Atlantic by the crew of the *MacKay Bennett*. He was wearing a light overcoat, black pants, and gray jacket. On his person was a gold watch with the letters "F.D.M." on a chain, glasses, two gold studs, a silver tablet bottle, 2 pounds and 10 shillings in gold, 8 shillings in silver, and a pocketbook.

His body was sent back to Boston where he was buried at East Bridgewater Central Cemetery.

Major Butt's body was never recovered, but a memorial marker exists at Arlington National Cemetery in the location where Butt had planned on being buried.

In one last tie to the Chicago area, a memorial was placed in the Ellipse in Washington, D.C., just south of the White House to honor both Major Butt and Mr. Millet. The designer of the monument worked with Millet during the construction of the White City and was none other than Daniel Chester French, who designed the iconic, sixty-five-foot-tall, gold leaf on plaster, "Republic" statue that towered over the east side of the Basin in the Court of Honor. French is more widely known for his statue of Abraham Lincoln at the Lincoln Memorial in Washington, D.C. and also designed the Marshall Field Monument at Graceland Cemetery in Chicago.

A twenty-four-foot gold-leaf-on-bronze replica of the "Republic" was dedicated on May 11, 1918, by French architect Henry Bacon to honor the 25th anniversary of the Exposition and the 100th Anniversary of Illinois becoming a state. It currently stands at the Hayes-Richards Circle in Jackson Park near the spot where the Administration Building of the Fair had once stood.

ANNIE KATE KELLY, ANNA McGOWAN, AND THE "ADDERGOOLE 14"

Not all Chicago links to the *Titanic* disaster involved people of world-wide notoriety. Many of the steerage passengers were merely immigrants attempting to start a new life in the United States.

One of those passengers was 20-year-old Anna Katherine Kelly, "Annie Kate," from Cuilmullagh, Lahardane, County Mayo, Ireland. Annie was one of the "Addergoole 14," a close-knit group of Irish immigrants from the Addergoole parish of which Cuilmullagh Lahardane was a part. Annie Kate (20), the youngest of the "14" Anna McGowan (17) and Bridget Delia McDermott (31), were the only three survivors of the group.

THE ADDERGOOLE 14

1. Katherine McGowan (cousin to Annie Kate)
2. Anna McGowan (Katherine McGowan's niece)
3. Anna Katherine "Annie Kate" Kelly (cousin to McGowans, Canavans, and Flynns)
4. John Bourke
5. Catherine Bourke (wife of John)
6. Mary Bourke (sister of John)
7. Mary Canavan (cousin to Patrick Canavan)
8. Patrick "Peter" Canavan
9. James Flynn
10. Bridget Donohoe
11. Nora Fleming
12. Mary Mangan
13. Bridget Mahon
14. Bridget Delia McDermott

I had the honor of working with Annie Kate's great-grandniece (Kathleen Herrebout) during the 2010 Federal Census. I also had the privilege of talking on the phone with Annie's grandniece (Mary Greene) as well.

Much of the information in this article comes from interviews with Annie's family, as well as a September 2011 article published by a great-nephew, John Kelly, and various articles of newspaper coverage from the time.

Annie was born on January 14, 1892, to John Kelly and Ellen Flaherty. Annie was the fourth oldest of nine children (eight girls and one boy). The children, in order of birth from oldest to youngest, were Margaret, Patrick, Bridget, Annie, Lilly, Ellie, Agnes, Emily, and Nora. Ellie died before reaching adulthood.

In October 1911, Katherine McGowan, who was living in Chicago, took her niece, Anna McGowan, to visit their relatives in Lahardane, County Mayo, Ireland. Katherine had recently emigrated to the U.S. and Anna McGowan had been born in Pennsylvania. Katherine's stories about America had been heard throughout the rural area, and by the time that Katherine was making her plans to go back to America, twelve other individuals from the area had decided to go with her on the return trip aboard the newest and most luxurious ship in the White Star Line, the RMS *Titanic*.

The night before the passengers had sailed, their families had thrown them a party. In Ireland, these were sometimes referred to as "American Wakes." It took a great deal of money for a trip to the States, and more often than not, travelers would not have the time or money for a return trip. Because of this, many people considered this the last time that they would ever see their America-bound relatives.

Annie Kate actually had relatives in Chicago awaiting her arrival: her eldest sister, Margaret Kelly Rowland, as well as two cousins, Anna and Mary Garvey.

According to John Kelly's article, a niece of Bridget Delia McDermott (Ms. Delia Melody of Ballina) related that Delia McDermott had a strange encounter the night before she had left for Queenstown. Delia was preparing for her departure by purchasing new clothes. One of her prized items was a sharp new hat. The evening before she left for Queenstown, as she was in Lahardane Village with friends, she was suddenly tapped on the shoulder. She turned around to see a mysterious little man dressed in black whom she thought was a traveler. As she reached in her purse to give the man a few pennies, he told her that he knew she was going on a long journey. He told her there would be a tragedy, but that she would be saved. As Delia turned back around to tell her friends, the little man disappeared. Her friends said that they hadn't seen anyone!

With anticipation, excitement, and heartache, the day of the departure of the "Addergoole 14" had come and they boarded the RMS *Titanic* on its maiden voyage to New York City. Queenstown (currently it has been renamed Cobh, "cove," the original name of the city) was actually the third boarding stop for the *Titanic*. It loaded passengers first at Southhampton, England, and a short time later in Cherbourg, France, and then finally in Queenstown. The *Titanic* left Queenstown bound for New York City at 1:30 p.m., April 11, 1912.

Once in the steerage section, Patrick Canavan, Annie's cousin of about the same age, and 43-year-old John Bourke explored the ship and happened to find a ladder that went from the steerage section all the way to the 1st Class Decks. (Little did they know how important this ladder would be later.)

At about 11:35 p.m. on Sunday night, April 14, 1912, the *Titanic* struck the infamous iceberg in the freezing cold North Atlantic and started to take on water. Patrick Canavan and John Bourke sensed something was wrong and gathered up the group. They escorted women and children up this ladder and nobody really knows how many were saved that night because of their selfless service and initial curiosity that led to the discovery of the ladder. The situation had become somewhat chaotic by the time many of the steerage (3rd class) passengers were aware of a problem and many of the group became separated. Anna McGowan and Delia McDermott ended up on the lifeboat boarding deck together, but Delia had forgotten her prized hat that she had bought before the trip. She raced back for her hat, and by the time she had returned, the lifeboat was being lowered. She actually jumped the fifteen feet from the rope ladder into the boat, and just as the strange little man in black had predicted, she was saved. Annie also became separated from the group, but as luck would have it, a young steward who had taken a liking to her during the trip found her looking lost and confused; he grasped her hand and led her to lifeboat #16. As she was approaching the boat, Catherine and Mary Bourke were climbing out because they'd heard that John Bourke would not be allowed in the boat. Annie was helped in. As lifeboat #16 was being lowered, Annie could see Patrick Canavan, John Bourke, his wife, Catherine, and his sister, Mary, standing at the railing. Patrick was holding his rosary and raised it to Annie as a blessing for safety as they watched her being lowered into the dark, cold waters.

When I talked to Annie's great-grandniece, she told me that her great-aunt very seldom talked about the *Titanic*. She did share some stories with her and she remembered how bitterly cold it was and how she prayed that if she made it out alive she would dedicate her life to the service of God. I'm sure Annie had some horrible memories of the *Titanic* that haunted her for many years.

I have read many of the survivor accounts and what seemed to be common in many of them was the roar of the screams that were heard as the ship was going down and then the eerie silence that followed shortly thereafter. I've heard of one survivor who could not go to a baseball game after the disaster because the roar of the cheers sounded too much like the roar of the screams heard that night.

It wouldn't be until 4:10 a.m. that the first *Titanic* survivor was rescued and brought aboard the *Carpathia*. The last person was brought aboard at about 9 a.m. When the *Carpathia* docked in New York, passengers were rushed through immigration and shipped off to nearby hospitals. Annie Kate and Anna McGowan both spent six weeks at St. Vincent Hospital and then were released to make the trip to Chicago with nothing but their nightgowns and coats. They did manage to get some leftover clothes and shoes and a train ticket to Chicago. Jane Addams had already been a pivotal figure in establishing a *Titanic* relief fund in Chicago and Dr. Mary O'Brien Porter of the Catholic Women's League Protectorate met Annie Kate and Anna McGowan and pleaded with Chicago Mayor Harrison to divert some of the *Titanic* relief funds from New York to help the two girls. Annie was still suffering from shock and exposure even six weeks later and a description of her condition was given in a *Chicago Tribune* article cited by John Kelly:

A nervous wreck as the result of her experiences on the *Titanic*, Miss Anna Kelly is at the home of her cousins, Anna and Mary Garvey, 306 Eugenia Street, with a physician constantly in attendance. Efforts are being made to save the reason of the young woman, who was one of the last steerage passengers to escape from the ill-fated boat. She has been unable to sleep, haunted by the wild scenes on the boat just before it went down, and is still suffering from the hours of exposure before she was picked up by the *Carpathia*. "Miss Kelly is a nervous wreck," said Dr. Thomas J. O'Malley, who is attending her. "I doubt she ever will completely recover her normal condition. Her life is in jeopardy now. Unless she can overcome her awful fear and terror at every sound, I fear for her life." Despite her condition, the young woman gave a graphic account of the wreck and the escape in one of the last lifeboats to leave the ship.

Anna did recover and joined Holy Name Cathedral Parish in Chicago and thanked God repeatedly for her rescue. It was there that she became acquainted with the Adrian Dominican Sisters. She remembered what she had talked to God about in the early morning hours of April 15, 1912, and on June 12, 1921, at the age of 29, she entered the convent in Adrian, Michigan. She took the name Sister Patrick Joseph after her older brother. She professed on August 12, 1924, at the age of 32 years, and made her final profession on June 19, 1933, at the age of 41.

Sister Pat loved Chicago and taught school for many years in the Chicago area, including Our Lady of Good Counsel, St. Phillip Neri, and St. Rita. She also taught at Ascension in Harvey, Illinois, and Visitation in Elmhurst, Illinois. She taught in other areas in Michigan and Iowa, as well, but whenever she was transferred, she always begged to come back to Chicago.

In the 1940s, she broke her hip, which resulted in a lifetime of limitation and pain, but it never slowed her down. In 1950, she made her first trip back to Ireland since that April in 1912. She was met by her older brother, Patrick, at Shannon Airport, was taken to the family farm in Cuillmullagh, and was reunited with many relatives and met new ones. She returned to Addergoole again in 1956.

Sister Pat taught until June 1969, when she retired to the motherhouse in Adrian, Michigan, and remained there until her death on December 18, 1969. She is buried on the grounds.

Kathleen, her great-grandniece remembered that she hardly ever talked about her experiences on the *Titanic,* but remembers her saying that she hated voting in Chicago early on because they would ask voters what boat they'd come to America on and it didn't matter whether a person said *Titanic* or *Carpathia;* it would always attract a crowd of people and she never liked to be the center of attention.

**29
Sister Patrick Joseph (Annie Kate Kelly) at the wedding of her niece, Mary Kelly Greene, February 8, 1964.** *Photograph courtesy of The Kelly Family.*

The doctor who first stated that Annie may not return to her normal condition was at least partially right. She probably turned out better than normal. She dedicated her life to the service of others because of the great gift of life that she was shown. She lived to be 77 years old after a very full life. Her cousin and hospital mate, Anna McGowan, passed away on January 30, 1990, as Anna F. Straube at the age of 92.

The Search for Peabody's Tomb and the Masochistic Monks?

If you were growing up on the west outskirts of the city of Chicago, it wouldn't be very long before you were introduced to the story of Peabody's Tomb. The story has been told many different ways by many different adolescents over the last seventy-five years or so. Most of them sound something like this:

> My big brother's girlfriend's best friend's brother told one of his friends that a group of them went to look for an old haunted mansion that was in the middle of the forest preserve a little bit west of here. The owner died a long time ago and was buried in a clear coffin that was filled with oil to keep his body from decaying. They say that the tomb is hidden somewhere on the property, some say a mausoleum, and is guarded by monks. If the monks catch you trying to find the tomb, they will take you into a chapel and force you to kneel on rice, marbles, or even broken glass! They force you to pray for the rest of the night and release you when morning comes. They even say that some kids have never come back!

Almost without fail someone tells of being chased by the monks and narrowly escapes being caught.

All myths, legends, ghost stories, and the like usually involve some fact mixed with some fiction. The question is, which is which? It doesn't take much of an investigator to figure out where the legend begins. It helps that people seem to have gotten the name right. Well, at least the last name anyway.

Francis Stuyvesant Peabody was born in Chicago to Francis B. Peabody and his wife, Harriet, in July 1859, in the family home at Rush and Erie Streets. His father, Francis B., an attorney, had just settled in Chicago from Maine two years earlier. Francis S. eventually graduated from Yale in the class of 1881 and made his way back to Chicago, where he worked as a messenger boy in the Merchants' Loan and Trust Company. He became interested in the coal business, and two years later, he formed Peabody, Daniels & Co. Daniels later disposed of his interest in the company and it became Peabody & Co. and was eventually incorporated. By 1894, Francis S. had grown his business to gross sales of $10,000,000 annually. Francis S. married May Henderson on November 23, 1887. May was the stepdaughter of John H. McAvoy, Board of Trade operator and founder and president of the McAvoy Brewing Company. Francis and May had two children: Stuyvesant "Jack" Peabody, born on August 7, 1888; and May, born April 28, 1891. Mrs. Peabody died of typhoid fever while traveling in the company of one of her best friends, Mrs. Florence Clark. She died on November 27, 1906, in Nice, France, approximately one week after contracting the disease. Her daughter, May, was 15½ and her son, Jack, was 18. Both of the children were away at school at the time.

Francis Stuyvesant Peabody.
Photograph provided by Mayslake Peabody Estate/Forest Preserve of DuPage County.

In 1908, Francis met Ms. Marian Bryant while on a trip in Europe and married her in 1909. F.S. Peabody was a great businessman, an avid sportsman, and active in politics and humanitarian causes. He lost a campaign for Cook County Sheriff in 1894, and had to remove himself from consideration as the Democratic nominee for the U.S. Senate

F.S. Peabody's daughter, May, and son, Stuyvesant "Jack" Peabody. *Photograph provided by Mayslake Peabody Estate/Forest Preserve of DuPage County.*

because of business concerns. He was a strong supporter of the Salvation Army during World War I and was awarded the degree of L.H.D. doctor of humane letters by the Temple University of Philadelphia, as well as being decorated by the King of Italy. From 1919 on, he concentrated on what was to be his retirement estate in Hinsdale (now Oak Brook), Illinois. He acquired 848 acres of land from various land owners in the area and hired the architect, Benjamin Marshall, to design what would eventually become a thirty-nine-room, Tudor-style mansion at a cost of about $750,000. This country estate, which he named "Mayslake Farm," became the premier show farm in the nation. It included two lakes, one of which he named Mayslake after his first wife and daughter, sixty buildings, elaborate stables, and an outdoor arena. He would invite many socialites to join him on drag hunts on the property. A drag hunt was a more humane way of fox hunting whereby a carcass or pelt of an animal was drug behind a horse and the dogs set loose to catch the scent of the drag rather than a live animal.

After one particular hunt on August 27, 1922, Mr. Peabody was missing. A search started immediately and the body of Mr. Peabody was found by the superintendent of the estate, Albert E. Cox. Mr. Peabody was lying beside his favorite horse, Dunbar, about 200 yards from the residence. Mr. Peabody was taken to the residence and physicians were summoned. Later, it was determined that Mr. Peabody did not fall from the horse, but dismounted and collapsed of an apparent heart attack. He had no history of heart disease and was in very good health.

The family did not wish to reside there any longer and the property was sold to the Franciscan Province of the Sacred Heart, Order of Friars Minor, in 1924, at a highly discounted price of $450,000. The family commissioned the Friars to build a monument to Francis Peabody. It would be a replica of the Portiuncula Chapel in Assisi, Italy, which takes its name from the "little portion" of land where St. Francis of Assisi received his call to serve the poor. The monument was originally located on the south side of Mayslake near the spot where Francis Peabody had died. The Franciscans converted the mansion to a retreat home and it became a popular spiritual respite from 1925 to 1991, with over 250,000 people spending weekends reflecting on biblical applications to life's difficulties.

It was during this time period that the legend of Peabody's Tomb flourished. I personally did not have any experiences with the Friars at Mayslake, but had been contacted by one after an article I had written a number of years ago. He is currently a lead customer specialist with a chemical company, but from 1971 to 1972 he was a Franciscan Brother (Order of Friars Minor). He made a point that they were Friars, not

Monks. That is why I always refer to them as Friars, with the exception of the title of this chapter, because that is how teenagers commonly referred to them. He went on to tell me that he was stationed at St. Paschal's Friary, which was built on Peabody's property. He had actually lived at the Peabody Mansion for about five months during that time. He went on to say that the Friars were not allowed on the grounds and especially the chapel at night because "the last thing the order wanted was for kids to actually run into any of the 'monks' down there, thus adding to the legends," of which they were well aware. He did remember that the chapel doors were chained shut most of the time and there were obvious signs of vandalism and attempts by kids of breaking into the doors. He did tell me of one encounter that I find very amusing and will quote him on this.

> October 4, 1971 was the Feast of Saint Francis and we were having a midnight mass at the chapel. I went there with a group at about 11 p.m. to get the chapel ready and set up candles inside, since there was no electricity to it. We had just set it up and came out of it and turned the corner to find a group of about ten teenagers coming towards us. They saw us and stopped dead and took off running. We could hear some of them yelling, 'We just wanted to see it.' And 'don't hurt us.' We all had a big laugh about it. We could just picture those kids going back to tell their friends that the monks chased them and tried to catch them to make them pray all night. Our mass was held at midnight and the building was re-locked and we were never allowed to go back to it at night at all.

I had a suspicion that many of the "masochistic monk" tales were made up and I know that there used to be a statue of a Friar on the grounds, which, at night, may have looked like a live person and scared many of the curious teenagers, but I have to be fair to the other side as well.

I have interviewed individuals who claimed to have had encounters with the Friars. One such interview was with a very well-respected member of the law enforcement community who is a retired chief of police in a western suburb of Chicago. He agreed to tell me the story as long as he could remain anonymous. The interview took place at the police station in February 2009.

He remembered very vividly that he and a group of friends from high school drove to the edge of the forest preserve and attempted to locate the tomb. He stated that the version of the legend he heard was that Peabody's see-through casket was inside a small chapel on the

Southern view of Mayslake Hall.

Northern view of Mayslake Hall.

grounds of the estate, but that there was a large stash of gold buried beneath his tomb. I asked if he had an encounter with the Friars who owned the property at the time and he stated that they were initially scared by what they thought was a monk, but later was determined to be the statue of a monk. I asked him why there was a statue of a monk and he said that there was a cemetery inside the grounds. (I had previously learned of the removal of many graves from the grounds at the time that the forest preserve had taken ownership, so it did make sense.) The second time they were startled, it was by actual monks who *did* chase them. He and another friend had gotten away, but another of their friends was not so lucky. When they had spoken to him the next day at school (yes, he did make it back in one piece) the friend

The Search for Peabody's Tomb and the Masochistic Monks?

had told of being apprehended by the monks and given the choice of kneeling on a broomstick (I had not heard the broomstick version) and praying or having the police called in. His friend chose to not have the police notified. His friend did tell them that it was only a very short period of time (15 minutes or so) and then he was released to continue the spread of the legend.

Eventually, the Friars sold off portions of the land to local real estate developers and the chapel, along with Mr. Peabody's remains, had to be relocated to the northeast side of the estate. In 1990, the Franciscans announced that they were going to sell their remaining acreage, which included Mayslake Hall, to a real estate developer who planned to raze the buildings and replace them with luxury homes. A massive campaign was undertaken, which resulted in a referendum that enabled the Du Page County Forest Preserve district to purchase the property in 1992.

There are also some more recent spine-chilling encounters. According to Richard Crowe's 2004 book, *Chicago's Street Guide to the Supernatural*, a Du Page County Forest Preserve ranger was spending the night in a wing of the big house and heard what sounded like a child bouncing a ball outside of her door. Of course, when the ranger investigated, nothing was found. This same incident occurred a number of times. Mr. Crowe also recounts information from a fiancé of a curator who moved in after the ranger was reassigned. The fiancé mentioned that when peering out of an upstairs window, she remembered seeing a small boy approximately eight or nine years old with a mop of curly brown hair. She recalled seeing this boy several times.

While the boy definitely doesn't fit the description of Francis Stuyvesant Peabody, there is now speculation that the boy could have been the result of an illicit affair between Mr. Peabody and a servant girl. Part of the reason for this speculation, according to Mr. Crowe's book, is the existence of a "mystery room" that contains a cedar wood closet and is secretly adjacent to the common servants' quarters.

I recently took a tour of the Mayslake Estate. The Mansion is currently under renovation, with money donated by private benefactors, as well as a grant that was received from Peabody Energy, St. Louis (the still extant company founded by Francis Peabody) in honor of their 125th anniversary. It was a magnificent home and while it is in need of renovation, the original woodwork was ornate and very beautiful.

The Portiuncula Chapel on the Mayslake Estate.

One thing I did notice was a secret passageway that had been left
ajar and was blocked off from the tour. It started in a room just off of
the west of the entrance foyer adjacent to the grand staircase that led
to the second floor. The entrance to the passageway at the ground
level was not hidden very well, but had the entrance to the passageway
been closed, it would have been very difficult to find because it looked
like a small storage closet. The narrow staircase that wound up to the
second floor exited through a wall in the personal library/sitting room
of Francis Peabody. From inside the library, you would not notice the
entrance leading down. It appeared as just another panel in the wall
adjacent to a bookshelf. It was very well made and you literally could
not see the gap in the opening when it was shut completely. I found
out (after closer inspection) that this was actually a secret passageway
within a secret passageway! If you happened to find the entranceway at
the top and walked down the stairway to the exit on the first floor, you

**View of the closed secret passage leading from the personal
library on the second floor of Mayslake Hall.**

might overlook the small shallow wine cabinet to your right. The entire cabinet pulled away and was a hinged door itself! I was told that it went down to a bomb-proof basement.

It seems that Mr. Peabody was very worried about the labor movement of his time and the violence that sometimes erupted as a result of the struggles during that movement. I'm sure that Mr. Peabody's psyche was personally affected by the Haymarket Affair of May 4, 1886 in Chicago. Also called the "Haymarket Riot," it resulted in the deaths of eight Chicago police officers and an untold number of civilians. It started as a rally in support of striking workers and took place only two years after Peabody started his coal business. It seems that he was worried about his family's well being and the idea of having hidden rooms or "panic rooms" during those times is not such a "paranoid" idea.

Currently the "big house" is being renovated and is being used to teach classes in the fine arts. They have many different public festivals during the year, including a Shakespeare festival that consists of outdoor

View of the open secret passage.

plays put on by the non-profit First Folio Theater, which also does a series of live Edgar Allan Poe performances at the mansion, as well as a very recent Halloween-themed special performance of "Searching for Peabody's Tomb," written by Chrissie Howorth, who is also an employee of the Forest Preserve District and actively involved in fundraising efforts.

So what about Peabody's remains? After a little poking around, I discovered that on October 23, 1991, the remains of Mr. Peabody, along with the brothers of the Friary, were removed from the property and re-interred at a local Catholic cemetery. He has a very simple flat stone and is lying next to his son, Stuyvesant "Jack," who passed away in 1946. They are the first and second graves in a plot dedicated to the Franciscan Order. I chose not to include the exact name and location of the cemetery because I did not want to invite any new generations of trespassers, but I did want to let any would-be "tomb raiders" know that there are no more graves at the "Peabody Estate."

However, if you don't believe that the bodies have been moved and you can't resist the urge to sneak in after dark, you won't have to deal with masochistic monks, but you *will* have to deal with the Du Page County Forest Preserve Police! You may end up wishing that you could just kneel on rice!

The simple stone of Francis Stuyvesant Peabody.

Voice of the Grimes Sisters' Killer?

Many years ago, I became interested in the unsolved 1956 murders of Chicago teenage sisters Barbara and Patricia Grimes. The crime interested me for a number of reasons. I was interested as a criminal investigator, as a researcher, and also as someone who appreciates the historical significance of the various aspects of the crime. This crime was one that struck terror into the hearts of not only parents of young children, but also in the hearts of the kids themselves. It really was a turning point in the amount of freedom that parents gave their children and brought a screeching halt to the all too false sense of security that parents and children had prior to this time period.

"The Big Three" (as I like to call them) crimes against children in the Chicago area were the cases of the Schuessler/Peterson boys, the Grimes sisters, and of Judith Mae Andersen. The bodies of 13-year-old John Schuessler, his 11-year-old brother, Anton Jr., and their 14-year-old friend, Robert Peterson, were found October 18, 1955, in the Robinson Woods forest preserve; the Grimes sisters, Barbara, 15, and Patricia, 13, were found January 22, 1957, on a lonely stretch of German Church Road in unincorporated Burr Ridge; and the dismembered body of 15-year-old Judith Mae Andersen was found in multiple steel oil barrels fished out of Montrose Harbor on August 22, 1957 and August 24, 1957.

**Mrs. Schuessler faints at the 1955 funeral of
her two murdered boys, John (13) and Anton Jr.
(11).** *Author's personal collection.*

These were three major cases involving the murders of teenagers in a very short period of time, even for Chicago. It was truly, in my opinion, the beginning of the end of innocence for Chicago's youth. I covered the Grimes case in detail in my first book, *Chicago's Haunt Detective* (Schiffer Publishing, 2011) and will only include a synopsis of the case and pertinent details as they relate to another less well-known case of teenage murder that, in my opinion, holds the answers to the as yet unsolved murders of the Grimes sisters. This would be the 1958 case of the murder of 15-year-old Bonnie Leigh Scott of Addison, Illinois.

Judith Mae Andersen's dismembered body is found in one of two drums fished out of Montrose Harbor, August 22, 1957. *Author's personal collection.*

But first, a brief history of the Grimes case.

On December 28, 1956, sisters Barbara and Patricia Grimes left their home at 3634 S. Damen Avenue in Chicago's "Back of the Yards" neighborhood at around 7:30 p.m. in order to see the movie, *Love Me Tender*, starring their one and only heart-throb, Elvis Presley. Of course, that is the way many teenage fans of Elvis were thinking at the time. They made their way, presumably by bus, to the since-demolished Brighton Theater at 4211 S. Archer Avenue in the Brighton Park Neighborhood. By all accounts, they did make it to the theater, but it is what happened after that remains an uncertainty. The girls did not return home at the expected time, and their mother, Loretta Grimes, checked with friends and neighbors who saw the girls at the theater, but could not vouch for their whereabouts after the movie was over. Loretta reported them to the Chicago Police Department as missing, but the police did not take the case seriously until about a week after their disappearance. They had initially told their mother that the girls were probably runaways or were out with boyfriends. Loretta did not once entertain any of those theories and neither did those close to the girls. They only took what money they needed for the movie and bus fare. They did not take any extra clothes with them and they had left all of their Christmas presents at home, including a cherished portable A.M. radio. Besides, they were very much homebodies and not prone to partying.

What eventually followed was a missing persons' case that made national news and Elvis himself was heard on the radio pleading for the girls, if they were listening, to return home as soon as they could. The FBI was even secretly involved due to some ransom notes that Loretta Grimes had received, but none of those turned out to be anything but hoaxes.

Then, on the afternoon of January 22, 1957, after a period of unseasonably mild temperatures, a man named Leonard Prescott, who lived in unincorporated Hinsdale, was driving east on German Church Road from County Line Road in the unincorporated area of Burr Ridge. He saw what he believed, or hoped to be, two mannequins lying just over the north guard rail where Devil's Creek crossed under German Church Road. At first he just passed it by on his way to a grocery store, but it really bothered him. He went back to his home to pick up his wife and they both went back to the location where they, unfortunately, discovered the unclothed bodies of two young girls. They reported their finding to the Willow Springs Police Department, and shortly after, everyone's worst fears were confirmed. They were indeed the corpses of 15-year-old Kelly High School student, Barbara Grimes, and her 13-year-old sister, Patricia.

What was once a missing persons' case of national attention was now an even more horrific murder investigation. Since the girls were first reported missing in Chicago, and the bodies were discovered in unincorporated Cook County, there was some initial tension between the Chicago P.D. and the Cook County Sheriff's Office, with the Cook County Sheriff's Office eventually taking lead investigative position. Many different departments were also volunteering services or were dragged into the investigation based on particulars of a constantly evolving case.

Various suspects were identified and ruled out, until a drifter by the name of Edward "Bennie" Bedwell was identified by his employer at the D&L Restaurant on Madison Street as having been with a male friend and two young girls who looked like the Grimes sisters. Bennie was a dishwasher with lower than average intellect and was picked up for three days of grueling interrogation in a motel owned by a Sheriff's Deputy. At the end of the three days, Bennie "confessed" to the crime, but was

The bodies of the Barbara and Patricia Grimes are covered with a tarp at the scene of their discovery on January 22, 1957. *Photograph courtesy of Bruce Beveridge.*

exonerated after the Coroner's report contradicted much of Bennie's confession. The case eventually went "cold" and to this day remains unsolved.

In my first book, I cover the case in more detail, but was unable to share information with the public that I had uncovered during my initial

Theresa, the older sister of Barbara and Patricia Grimes, tries to comfort her mother, Loretta, after finding out the news of the discovery of the girls' bodies. *Author's personal collection.*

research on the Grimes case. Before I had turned in my manuscript for the first book, I had come across a case that was similar to the Grimes case and there exists some physical and circumstantial evidence that points to a particular person who, in my opinion, could very well be the person responsible for the deaths of Lorreta Grimes' teenage daughters.

THE MURDER OF BONNIE LEIGH SCOTT

Bonnie Leigh Scott was a 15-year-old sophomore at York High School and from all accounts had somewhat of a dysfunctional upbringing. She was living at 112 Normandy Drive in Addison with her aunt and uncle, Mr. and Mrs. Robert H. Schwolow, as well as her grandmother, Mrs. Doris Hitchins, who was her legal guardian. Her father, Guy, was reportedly a disabled veteran living on the West Coast, while her mother, Marilyn, was a patient at the Elgin State Mental Hospital. Bonnie reportedly had trouble in school and had run away from home at least once and was gone for almost two days. She definitely fit the mold of a very vulnerable, impressionable young girl who might be starving for affection and therefore an easy target for a child predator.

Charles Melquist was born on May 3, 1937, and was the son of Elmer Melquist and Hazel Smith. In 1958, he was living with his sister and parents at 655 Yale Street in Villa Park, Illinois. He had a short stint in the military and was a past student at Willowbrook High School.

Melquist met Bonnie Scott in the summer of 1957 at a carnival when Melquist was roughly 20 years old and Bonnie was 14. He had become a "big brother" figure to Bonnie and considered her a good friend. On the evening of September 22, 1958, Bonnie Leigh Scott failed to come home. Her grandmother contacted the Addison police and they started interviewing Bonnie's friends. Melquist was more than willing to help in whatever way he could to find Bonnie. He told police and reporters that when he originally met Bonnie, about 1½ years prior, that he had thought she was 17 years old. He had said that he considered her a "nice, but mixed-up kid" and they dated about three times. It wasn't until they visited her mother at the Elgin State Mental Hospital that he found out that she was only 14 years old. He told police of a phone call that Bonnie made to him at his home in Villa Park, with her saying that she was having problems with a boyfriend who was making unwelcome sexual advances. He told police that she often called him when she had personal problems. It was later that night when Melquist claimed to have received a phone call from a male that he didn't recognize claiming to be Scott's boyfriend and that she had jumped out of his car at Route 66 and Mannheim. (That intersection would be Joliet Road and La Grange Road today.) The male told Melquist that Scott wanted Melquist to pick her up. The Addison police thought Melquist's story was a little fabricated, but they had nothing else to go on.

They continued interviewing friends and relatives, and it was the interviews they conducted at the 4D Restaurant at 12 E. Lake Street in Addison that added another inconsistency to Melquist's story. Police interviewed a waitress and four teenage boys who were with Bonnie on the night she disappeared. The waitress stated that the five were eating there, and after they'd finished, they went into the parking lot at about 7:30 p.m. and danced in the lot until about 8 p.m. or later to the music from the boys' car. The boys then left after Bonnie refused a ride from them. That would make it highly unlikely that Bonnie would have made an 8:15 p.m. phone call to Melquist complaining about sexual advances of a boyfriend.

For the next week, Melquist took Bonnie's grandmother out in his vehicle to search the area of Route 66 and La Grange Road, as well as driving around the neighborhood looking for any trace of Bonnie.

On Saturday, November 15th, a group of Boy Scouts from Cicero, Illinois, led by Edward Zatas of 5322 W. 30th Place, were on a nature hike in the forest preserves of Palos Hills when they came upon the decapitated corpse of a female that was badly decomposed. The body was found about 250 feet south of 95th Street on the west side of La Grange Road, about 15 feet off the road and very close to the Suttonbush Slough. At first police believed it could be the body of a newspaperwoman named Mollie Zelko who had disappeared 13 months prior to the discovery. The body weighed between 110 and 120 pounds, was about 5 feet 5 inches in height, with reddish-brown hair and silver painted nails.

Bonnie Scott's grandmother, Mrs. Hitchins, called the Addison police after she found out that a body had been discovered and spoke with Chief Nels Anderson and Sgt. William Deveaney. She asked them if the body that was found could be that of her granddaughter's. Mrs. Hitchins told them that if they spoke with Dr. P.D. Grimes in Elmhurst that he could compare the dental records of Bonnie to the dental work of the dead girl. Sgt. Deveaney and his partner, William Craig started contacting all known friends of Bonnie and came across the name of Charles Melquist, who they remembered was wanting to be very helpful in the case, and the location of where the victim was found was not too far from the location where the strange caller to Melquist said Bonnie had jumped from his car.

The Addison P.D. found Melquist at 11:30 p.m. on November 16th, and they requested him to come to the Addison P.D. because they had some questions regarding the murder of Bonnie Leigh Scott. Melquist went to the police station and spoke with Sergeant Deveaney. Deveaney questioned Melquist until about 3:15 a.m. on the 17th and then Chief Anderson himself gave Melquist a ride home to Villa Park. As they sat in the driveway, Melquist shared with Chief Anderson that he'd planned on applying to the Du Page County Sheriff's Police on November 25th and was hoping that his being questioned in the Scott case wouldn't hinder his chances of becoming a deputy. They asked Melquist if he could come back at 10 a.m. and Melquist cooperated, returning with his father, Elmer, and actually requested to be given a polygraph (lie detector test). A portable lie test, supplied by the Cook County Sheriff's Police, was administered to Melquist at the Addison P.D. by operator George Haney, with results indicating that Melquist was being deceptive. Melquist then voluntarily accompanied police officers to the offices of John Reid at 600 N. Michigan Avenue. (I know for a fact that for someone planning on being deceptive, this is the last place they would want to go. John E. Reid is one of the pioneers on deception detection and is the national, if not world, authority on the art of interviewing and interrogation, even today. As a criminal investigator, I was taught by the Reid Institute and was also taught the Reid method in many, if not all, of my interview and interrogation classes as part of my training. In 1945, he patented the "Reid Polygraph" that not only measured heart rate, respiration, blood pressure, and perspiration, but also muscular movements in the forearms, thighs, and feet.) Before the end of the polygraph, Melquist was confessing in great detail how he went about murdering and disposing of the body of Bonnie Leigh Scott.

After the Reid offices, Melquist went with officers to the offices of Frank Ferlic, the Cook County State's Attorney, where he gave a more detailed confession. Feric stated that Melquist was unemotional during the questioning, but was concerned about how his parents might be reacting. At approximately 11 p.m. on the same day, Melquist was taken from the State's Attorney's office of Cook County to the Bedford Park Police Station in Bedford Park, Illinois, by Chief Smith of the Cook County Sheriff's Police and John Roche, Supervising Captain of the Cook County Sheriff's Department. After 10 a.m. on November 18th, Chief of Police Holler of the Villa Park P.D. and deputy sheriffs Mertes and Lang of Du Page County went to the Cook County Sheriff's Office in Bedford Park to transport Melquist to the Villa Park P.D. Melquist was transported in Smith's vehicle and arrived at the Villa Park P.D. at about 11 a.m., where Melquist was served with an arrest warrant for the murder of Bonnie Leigh Scott. He was transported to the Du Page County Jail where Elmer Melquist and Melquist's attorney, Robert McDonnell, were trying to get a writ of habeas corpus, but murder charges had already been filed.

Melquist's Confession

Melquist told police that, on September 22nd, he'd picked up Bonnie at her home in Addison and drove to the driveway of his home on Yale in Villa Park at around 8 p.m. He said that they were being playful and that he grabbed a pink satin throw pillow and pressed it against her face. "I just pulled out the pillow and held it over her head," he said. "I held it too long and she smothered. I saw she was not moving." He then stripped off her clothes and stuffed them under his front seat. He drove the body to the area of La Grange Road and 95th Street where he stated he pushed the body across the guard rail just like a sack. "She was lying

Charles Leroy Melquist listens to the guilty verdict in the case of the murder of Bonnie Leigh Scott. He was sentenced to 99 years, but only served a small portion of that time. *Author's personal collection.*

on her back. I dragged her by the feet down the embankment, 15 feet to this small thicket. Then I left." Melquist returned home and for days thought that he must have dreamt the whole thing and couldn't believe that he could have killed Bonnie. He said that he had to go back to determine if she was there or if it had all been a dream. He returned on Friday, September 16th, and verified that there was a body and that he had not dreamt the whole affair. He said that he returned to the scene about a month later and took with him a four-inch butcher knife and a pitchfork and that he intended to bury her with, but when he saw the body again, he had an overwhelming "urge to cut." He took the knife and severed Bonnie's head and then picked it up and threw it about 20 yards from the body. He then turned the knife to the torso and just

Convicted murderer, Charles Leroy Melquist, is led to jail by Sheriff Larry Springborn and Chief Deputy Sheriff Herb Mertes of the DuPage County Sheriff's Office after he was found guilty of murdering 15-year-old Bonnie Leigh Scott. *Author's personal collection.*

started slashing. He stated he returned to the body a third time, but was scared away by some people walking nearby. It was then, and only then, when he threw the knife out of his vehicle on the east side of La Grange Road, north of 95th Street, and drove to the area of Irving Park and Elmhurst Road, where he found a bonfire and he threw Bonnie's clothes in to burn. If this was true, then Bonnie's clothes were in the vehicle when the Addison P.D. had first questioned Melquist and they were in the vehicle when Melquist transported Bonnie's grandmother around the communities looking for traces of the missing girl.

What About the Grimes Girls?

The Cook County Sheriff's Department and Chicago P.D. were not blind to the fact that there were some startling similarities between the Grimes case of 1956 and the Scott case of 1958. Unfortunately, Melquist's attorney blocked any chance that law enforcement had to interview Melquist about the Grimes case or the other child murder cases that were on their plates. They had a strong case against Melquist and he was found guilty in May of 1959 and sentenced to 99 years in prison. I believe, at that point, people felt justice was done and Melquist would spend the rest of his life in prison; unfortunately that wouldn't be the case. At some point, and as best I can gather, he was released from prison prior to 1970, thereby only spending a little over 10 years in prison. It was at this time, May 2010, that I had the opportunity to share information on Melquist with the Chicago P.D. cold case unit and the Cook County State's Attorney's Office. I gave the following reasons why I believed Charles Melquist to be a prime suspect in the murders of Barbara and Patricia Grimes:

Similarities in Method of Death and Disposal of Body

The results of the autopsies of Barbara and Patricia failed to find a cause of death of the girls with the exception of exposure to the elements or possible suffocation. Charles Melquist admitted to killing Bonnie Leigh Scott by suffocating her with a pillow. He then dropped the unclothed body of Bonnie Leigh Scott just off of the road, over the guardrail, at approximately 95th and La Grange Road about three miles from where the Grimes girls' bodies were dumped in the exact same fashion. The clothing of the Grimes girls and those of Bonnie Leigh Scott was never discovered. Melquist was known to be a student of Judo and could render someone unconscious fairly easily. He was also accused by former girlfriends of trying to choke them.

Psychiatric Opinion

An article written by Robert Wiedrich appeared in the *Chicago Tribune* on November 20, 1958, quoting opinions from Dr. Paul Hletko, chief medical officer of the State Welfare Department. In the article Dr.

Hletko stated, "I think that when the Grimes killer is found he will be the same type of person as Charles Melquist." He also goes on to state that Melquist saw himself as a "Lady's Man" with long sideburns, carefully waved hair, and the hot-rod manner in which he drove his car all point to the same type of individual. He stated that Melquist had fantasies of throwing naked women into whirling blades to destroy them and the fact that he returned to the body of Bonnie Leigh Scott to slash it supported the doctor's theory that Melquist was an obsessive compulsive who associated sex with something horrible. This theory also goes to explain the next point.

Inexplicable Puncture Wounds

on Patricia Grimes' Chest

As a result of the autopsy of the Grimes girls, a cause of death was not found, although "exposure" is listed as the official cause of death. There were, however, three puncture wounds found on the chest of Patricia who was lying on top of her sister face up. The puncture wounds appeared to have been inflicted by an ice pick or similar weapon, but the wounds were only about ¾ of an inch deep, which was not deep enough to have been fatal. As with Melquist's M.O., if he were to usually return to the scene of the crime to mutilate the body because of some "urge" that he had mentioned in his confession, he would have suffered from this same "urge" if he were responsible for the murder of the Grimes sisters. According to reports of searches conducted on Melquist's house and vehicle, a three-pronged garden fork was found in the trunk of Melquist's vehicle. If Melquist returned to the bodies of the Grimes sisters, there would have been one big difference between what he would have found from their bodies and Scott's. Scott's body was disposed of in September and discovered in mid-November. The Grimes girls went missing at the end of December and their bodies were found in late January. Anyone who has lived in Chicago during the winter knows how cold it can get in January, and without a doubt, Melquist would have encountered frozen bodies. If Melquist would have used an ice pick or even the three-pronged garden fork to slash the Grimes girls, he would have likely started with the girl on top (Patricia) and met with a solid mass. Anyone who has ever tried to cut into a frozen beef roast knows that the knife will not go in far, hence the shallow wounds.

MELQUIST WAS FAMILIAR WITH THE AREA

WHERE THE GRIMES GIRLS WERE FOUND

I am still of the opinion that Melquist may not have acted completely alone in the Grimes case because I find it difficult to believe that he could have killed both girls without leaving marks, even if he *was* a "judo expert." In the Grimes case, a man by the name of Walter Kranz had called the police before the girls were found murdered and stated that the police would find their bodies at Sante Fe Park. Santa Fe Park or Santa Fe Raceway was only a three-minute drive due south of the area where the Grimes girls were found and Charles Melquist told investigators that he frequently went to races at the park. Also, the body of Bonnie Leigh Scott was found roughly the same distance from Santa Fe Park, but in a different direction. Walter Kranz was given a lie detector test and passed with the exception of one question and that one question was whether he had ever seen the Grimes girls alive! It was conceivable that if Kranz and Melquist frequented the same area, he could have left one of the girls with Kranz while he murdered the other and then went back to get the other girl under the guise of joining back up with her sister. In that way, Melquist would only have had to deal with one of the girls at a time and Kranz may not have been involved in the murder, but Santa Fe Park may have been the last place that Kranz saw the girls alive and figured that was where the bodies would have been found. Even if he wasn't directly involved in the murder, he still may have been reluctant to go to the police knowing that he very easily could have been implicated in the murder. But he may have still had some internal guilt about having seen the girls at Santa Fe Park shortly before they were reported missing and could think of no other excuse than "having a psychic dream," which is what he originally told investigators when he made that anonymous phone call to the police before the girls' bodies were found.

PHONE NUMBERS OF NEIGHBORS OF THE GRIMES GIRLS

WERE FOUND IN MELQUIST'S PHONE LIST

During a search of Melquist's house at 655 Yale in Villa Park, investigators found the phone numbers of numerous girls around the same age as Bonnie Leigh Scott and the phone numbers of two neighbors of the Grimes girls. The police found the phone numbers of Sharon Blomberg, 15, of 1406 W. Marquette Road who formerly lived at 3332 Archer Avenue, which was only two blocks from the Grimes sisters, and Diane Prunty, 15, of 3949 S. Rockwell Street, who used to live at 4331 S. Maplewood, which was only a half-mile trek through McKinley Park to where the Grimes sisters lived. They also stated that they commonly visited a sweets shop at 35th and Archer that the Grimes girls also frequented, swam in McKinley Park close to where the girls lived, and had gone to the Brighton Theater where the girls watched *Love Me Tender* the night they disappeared.

LORETTA GRIMES RECOGNIZED A VOICE

Loretta Grimes, mother of the Grimes girls, received a great many prank calls and letters, both before and after the bodies of her girls were found. Many of these phone calls and letters were very cruel with some stating that the girls were immoral and got what was coming to them. In May of 1957, about three months after the girls' bodies were discovered, Loretta received a call that she said she would never forget. The male caller stated that he knew who killed her girls and that he had been the one who undressed them. He stated, "I know something about your little girl (Barbara was the older, but smaller one) that no one else knows but you—not even the police. The smaller girl's toes were crossed on both of her feet." This was a little-known deformity that Barbara had, and after revealing that information, the caller laughed cruelly.

The day after the Scott body was found, and before anyone knew the identity of the girl, Loretta Grimes received another phone call. She was positive that the voice of the man was the same voice of the caller back in May. The caller boasted, "I committed another perfect crime. This is another one those cops won't solve and they're not going to hook it onto Bedwell or to Barry Cook." He laughed after making the statement about Bedwell and Barry Cook who was a suspect, because Bedwell was a Grimes suspect and Cook was a suspect in the Judith Mae Andersen case; and then he hung up. Loretta definitely recognized the voice of the caller in both cases and she was positive it was the same person. She said that she could never forget his voice!

A New Witness Comes Forward!

About a year after my first book came out, I had been trading emails with Stephan Benzkofer of the *Chicago Tribune* who writes a special column in the paper entitled "Chicago Flashback." The column highlights a past Chicago event and discusses the *Tribune's* coverage of the historic event with photos and stories that had originally run in the paper. Stephan had emailed me asking if I would have any ideas for a January column and I had suggested the Grimes sisters, since their bodies were discovered on January 22nd of 1957. He ran the column in the Sunday, January 22, 2012 edition of the paper and listed my contact information at the end of the article for suggesting it. I received an email on January 27, 2012, from a woman whose name I would like to keep private for obvious reasons. In the email, she explained how after she had seen Benzkofer's article, it brought back painful memories of her childhood. She had been abducted with the Grimes sisters that December 28th night in 1956! I contacted the Chicago P.D. cold case guys and informed them of the email. They, like myself, thought that there was always the chance that the person on the other end of the email was making up the story or might not be in their right state of mind. I asked them if they would mind me setting up a meeting with her to discuss her information and get a read on her state of mind and they actually appreciated the help, since it is very difficult to get authorization to expend resources on a fifty-six-year-old case. I set up a meeting with the woman and had my wife come along as well. She was a very nice woman and very much in her right state of mind. She seemed very intelligent and had a fascinating life up to this point. We picked her up at her home and went to lunch at a local diner where she told of her harrowing experience with Barbara and Patricia Grimes.

She was a friend of Barbara Grimes because they both attended Kelly High School and she met up with the girls at the Brighton Theater that night. They expected it to be a full house and there was a long line at the ticket booth. The woman in the ticket booth had a red beehive-style hairdo with horned-rimmed glasses and she was holding a roll of tickets. She tore off the tickets for the three of them and then she remembers her shaking her head as they walked by to meet the guy who would tear the tickets in half. The girls would meet in the bathroom before the show and talk with friends from school or the neighborhood. There really wasn't much to do in the bathroom but smoke and gossip or you could weigh yourself for a penny and the scale would kick out a piece of paper with your fortune. She smiled when she told us this and said, "We were easily amused back then."

Shortly before the movie started, they walked up to find three seats together, which, by this time, was pretty difficult, but they managed to find them in about the middle of the theater. After the movie was over, Barbara and Patricia went back down to the bathroom and she stayed to watch a cartoon that they would usually show after each movie. Not many of the kids stayed to watch the cartoon, so there was plenty of seating available.

Suddenly a man sat down next to her, which she thought was really odd, since there were so many seats available. It made her extremely nervous and she purposely looked straight forward at the cartoon and tried to ignore him. After about a minute he reached for her hand and brought it into his lap! At this point, she was terrified and didn't know what to do. He held her hand in his lap for a minute or two and then she pulled away. He asked her if she wanted any soda or candy and she just shook her head no. After what seemed like an eternity, she saw Barbara and Patricia heading back towards their seats and the guy got up and walked away.

All three girls left the theater together and started walking down Archer Avenue. She remembered that it was freezing and very uncomfortable. After a block or two, a big black car pulled up and a man's voice said, "Its cold outside! You girls want a ride?" Patricia, being the more outgoing of the two girls, jumped into the back seat first with Barbara muttering something to her and she climbed in last, shutting the car door as it pulled away. All three of them were in the back seat and she made a point to tell the guy that she lived down Archer Avenue and pointed in the direction. As they passed Kelly High School, he asked if any of the girls went there, and one of the sisters giggled. He couldn't hear them so he asked them what they said, but neither girl answered. As they passed the ice cream place that was a local hangout, the car took a quick right down Pershing and then a quick left into the alley. She was a little frightened by this quick maneuver, but was glad because it just happened to be the alley on the block where she lived. The driver had to slow down for potholes and when he almost came to a complete stop to avoid a larger rut, she opened up the back door and jumped out. The car kept moving and the door shut. She remembered stopping to talk to her neighbor who was outside in his backyard taking out the garbage and she watched the car speed up down the alley and out of sight. She didn't even

Voice of the Grimes Sisters' Killer?

believe that the guy ever knew that she had gotten out of the car. She didn't have a good feeling about the situation, and when she was finished talking with the neighbor, she went inside and went to bed.

She returned to school after the Christmas break and learned that the Grimes girls never made it home after the movie. A friend of hers pointed out the girls' older sister, Theresa Grimes, who was a senior and she remembered having a nauseated feeling in her stomach every time she saw Theresa because she had never told a soul about being with her sisters that night at the theater and being in the car with them.

A couple of days later, after she had gotten home from school, she heard a knock at the door and when she answered it, she saw a large man who said he was a detective with the Chicago Police Department. He showed her his badge and mentioned to her that he was there because a neighbor had called the police to tell them that he had seen her getting out of a black car rather quickly the night the girls disappeared. She remembered that she was desperately trying to hide the fact that she was scared out of her wits and calmly told the police officer, "The neighbor must be mistaken because it wasn't me and besides my parents do not allow me to accept rides from strangers." She felt shocked that he accepted her answer and thanked her as he scribbled some notes down on his pad and walked away.

She told me that she has lived with regret her entire life for not telling anyone what she knew about the sisters that night, but that she was only 14 at the time and scared out of her wits. She was so happy when her family decided to move by the spring of 1957 and she didn't have to face Theresa Grimes in school anymore. She also told me that she had suffered recurring nightmares for many years afterwards, in which she is walking down Archer Avenue late at night when a large black car pulls up alongside of her traveling at the same rate of speed as her. She runs down a number of alleys to avoid the car and then notices that the driver is now chasing her on foot. He catches up with her in the doorway of a building and starts savagely beating her until she is almost unconscious. The man drags her limp body back to his car, opens the trunk, and throws her in, and then everything goes black as he slams the trunk shut!

I asked her if she would be willing to talk to the police about this and she said that she would be willing, but didn't know how much help she could be. I asked her if she would be able to recognize anyone from photographs as the person who was driving the car that night, but she said she only saw him from the side when he was talking to them from the front seat. I asked her if she thought the guy who sat down next to her in the movie was the same guy driving the car and she said that she is positive it was the same guy because he had a very distinctive voice! That statement hit me like a ton of bricks because Loretta Grimes had said the same thing about the person who called her in May of 1957 and in November of 1958 after the Scott girl was found.

As of the writing of this, the Chicago P.D. and this woman have not yet set up a time to sit down together and Charles Melquist died of lung cancer on June 26, 2010, but I have not given up hope that this case can be put to rest. I am in the process of attempting to see what evidence may still remain locked up somewhere from the Scott case of 1958, and while Charles Melquist is gone and cremated, I am aware that after he was released from prison he married and had children of his own. I am not releasing any of the information about his family because I want to respect their privacy, but I am hoping that if there is any chance of recovering any DNA-related evidence from a Cook County Sheriff's Department locker and the Melquist family is willing to cooperate, than there may be a slight chance that this case could be brought to some kind of conclusion. I am also hoping that by publishing this chapter there also may be an old associate or friend of Charles Melquist who might remember him mentioning something about two teenage girls from the McKinley Park neighborhood.

The Tonic Room Witch

I have to say, I came across this little tidbit of Chicago history completely by accident, coincidence, or fate, depending on your viewpoint. A couple of years ago, I was researching the legendary vanishing hitchhiker of the southwest side, "Resurrection Mary," when I came across a band called "Resurrection Larry." I loved the play on words and eventually got to be friends with the members of the band and even found out that James Lang, vocals and keyboards, was also a fan of one of my favorite local Chicago celebrities, Rich Koz, who has for a great number of years been the TV horror host "Svengoolie." I don't think I have ever seen Jim play a gig without some reference, usually a t-shirt, to "Sven."

One day, Jim let me know that "Rez Larry" (actually there is no band member by the name of Larry) was going to play at the Tonic Room at 2447 N. Halsted Street in Chicago. He also mentioned that rumor had it that the place was haunted. I admit that I didn't know much about the Tonic Room, but I had heard the location mentioned a number of times and had read an Internet post by Michael Kleen that listed it as one of Illinois's top ten haunted bars. I thought its history would be a cool project to investigate.

I had read several online accounts of the bar possibly being haunted because it was a "speakeasy" during Prohibition and there possibly could have been some mob "hits" at the place, but I couldn't find a reference to any such activity there. Of course, speakeasy's were a dime a dozen during the Prohibition era. My experience has been that bars *before* Prohibition were bars *during* Prohibition; they were usually just listed as entertainment companies. I had also heard that there may have been ritual murders there at some point, but couldn't find any deaths associated with the location at all. What I did find, I thought was extremely interesting.

Starting in January of 1969, what is now the Tonic Room was known as "El-Sabarum." A man by the name of Frederic De'Arechaga was the owner of the shop that catered to those interested in various facets of the occult. De'Arechaga considered himself to be a "Pontifus Maximus" in the Sabaean Religious Order (SRO) that he founded, and within the confines of the store which sold amulets, herbs, incense, goat hooves, voodoo beads, togas, jet stones to absorb bad spells, and ceremonial daggers, was his Temple of Saba. It was also known as "The Temple of the Moon." In the book *Popular Witchcraft—Straight from the Witch's Mouth* (University of Wisconsin Press, 2004), author Dr. Jack Fritscher interviewed De'Arechaga at "El-Sabarum" on September 20, 1969. According to the interview, De'Arechaga considered himself to be a "hereditary witch," receiving his gift from his mother who oversaw the Sabaean Order from a location at 3221 Sheffield. He also told Fritscher that he was bisexual and said:

> When modern witch hunters go out looking for witches or warlocks or whatever you want to call them, ask them a couple of questions. Most witches are full of crap. Make them put it on the line. Ask them if they're bisexual. If they're not, it's a giveaway."

He told a *Chicago Tribune* reporter that he had opened the shop in an effort to continue his mother's work after her death on August 4, 1969. He actually somewhat attributed his mother's death in 1969 to the Apollo Moon landing because much of her energy she received from the moon and that the landing had somehow caused injury to her. A 1970 *Chicago Tribune* article written by Mary Daniels described De'Arechaga's temple as being in the back of the store and containing Grecian pillars, red gauzy veils, cushions, and cooing pigeons.

He chose the name "El-Sabarum" because he said that it meant "of many gods." He considered himself to be of the "Old Religion"

The Tonic Room was the site of the "El-Sabarum" occult store and also the Sabaen Temple of the Moon.

and that Christians, Jews, and Muslims merely practiced degenerated versions of the "Old Religion." He even viewed Satanists as merely degenerates of the Catholic faith. De'Arechaga did not see a reason to delineate between "black" or "white" witches and the idea that there was good or bad in magic was something dreamed up mainly by the monotheistic religions. However, he did make somewhat of an ominous comment during Fritscher's interview when he stated:

> In my store I cease to sell certain things when another shop begins to handle the item. I do this out of respect to the other person. I thank the gods that other people have done this in turn for me. Some, however, purposely imitate what I do because they've got to get in on the bandwagon. They have no respect. They usually don't know what they're doing and they usually close up quite suddenly and quite mysteriously—ha!—if you know what I mean.

After the release of the movie *The Exorcist* on December 26, 1973, De'Arechaga told a *Tribune* reporter that he was being "plagued by an adverse public image." He reported that Christians had tried to exorcise the store out of the neighborhood, people would cross themselves passing by the store, or would even cross the street to avoid passing too close. He told the reporter that dogs would actually stop and walk carefully around the blue pentacles that he had painted on the sidewalk outside the store and that dead cats had been thrown through his front windows.

I wanted to get a chance to meet with the owners of the bar to see if there was anything remaining of the El-Sabarum or if they knew of the history and could add anything to what I had unearthed. I made contact with Tom Waits (co-owner with his father) of the Tonic Room and he was very accommodating. Tom was a great guy and very interested in the history of the building. He and his father had purchased the building in 2002 when it was the "Jub Jub" club. The Jub Jub Club existed for about 4½ years, and prior to that, the place was known as "The Everleigh Club," started by Michael Schuba. Michael later opened "Schuba's" with his brother, Chris, in the building at Belmont and Southport that was formerly Gaspar's. I gave him a summary of what I had discovered so far on the history of the building and he said that it all made sense and that it was probably the Schubas who purchased the building after De'Arechaga had moved on. I was a little disappointed that there were no remnants of Grecian columns or velvet curtains, but he did take me into the basement of the building and showed me a huge red pentagram that seemingly had been painted on the floor before the current walls were built because it spanned the size of two adjacent rooms. He also showed me some Egyptian-style murals that were painted on the ceiling and had been covered crudely by a seemingly quick-and-dirty wall-board covering. It appeared that there were more murals, but we obviously couldn't damage the existing ceiling to try to investigate. He showed me a rusted iron dagger that a friend named Charlie had found when they were digging out in the basement window wells for some improvement project. The dagger was pretty ominous in that it was rusted and had a skull decoration on the handle. The knife had been buried point down, right outside the window of the basement room with the red pentagram.

Tom said that he had never been told about the "El-Sabarum" or the "Temple of the Moon," but had suspected there was some sort of pagan worship going on, given the dagger, pentagram, and Egyptian murals. I asked him if there were any strange happenings at the bar that he couldn't explain and he then shared with me a story that

The barred grate covering the window well where a ritual knife was found buried by Tonic Room employees.

actually bothered him very much, and being a former investigator, I am pretty in tune with a "real" vs. "made-up" story.

Tom went on to tell me a tale about the pentagram in the basement. He mentioned that two employees of the bar, "Joey" and "Jack," were in the bar late one night and had been drinking a bit. They were both fairly new: Jack was the door guy and Joey worked behind the bar. They had gone to the basement to turn off the lights to close up for the night and they were goofing around, with the lights off, more or less taunting whatever spirits might be in the bar, when they both heard a noise they couldn't quite explain. It scared them to the point that they ran up the stairs and quickly left for the night. The very next night, Joey came back to work and was not drinking at all. He started to feel terrible. He felt so light-headed and sick that he had to leave the bar and went downstairs where he sat on the floor in the office on top of the painted pentagram. Mike D., one of Tom's friends who is in the bar quite a bit, was wondering about Joey because

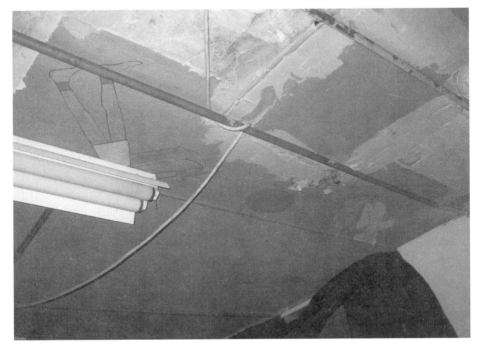

**Remnants of an Egyptian-style mural discovered
under a drywall ceiling in the basement of the
Tonic Room.**

he hadn't seen him in a while. He went downstairs to check on him
and Joey could not move. Joey said that he was literally paralyzed
and could not move off of the pentagram! Mike D. had to physically
pick Joey up, help him get upstairs, and take him straight to the
emergency room. The doctors could not come up with a reason for
Joey's symptoms or temporary paralysis. Joey immediately contacted
Tom and told him that there was no way that he could come back to
the Tonic Room to work. Tom said that, to his knowledge, Joey had
never had the symptoms before or since that incident.

While Tom embraced the history of the place that made it very
unique, he made it very clear that he did not want to spread rumors
about the place that couldn't be substantiated. He said that he had
been contacted by an individual who wanted to hold tours out of the
bar based on a séance that he had held there and came up with the
name of a "Mary Haggerty" who this person said had more than likely
died in the building. Tom said that he was not happy with the idea,

Remnants of a red pentacle painted on the floor of the basement from the time of the "El-Sabarum."

since the Haggerty story could not be substantiated. He was absolutely sure about the incident with Joey and that is one reason that he feels that he needs to have respect for whatever remains in the building and respectful of the history of the building. He also felt that since the dagger was found in the building, that it should remain in the building, and it is there to this day.

I found the story and history of the place fascinating and I am not any type of expert on pagan religions or witchcraft, so I called on Dr. Nefer Khepri out of Houston, Texas. Dr. Khepri is a published author in academia with a Ph.D, a professional Reader with over twenty-five years experience, a practicing Wiccan high priestess, and a Reiki Master teacher. She keeps an online presence at http://magickal-musings.com. I wanted to see if she could try to make sense of what remained of the El-Sabarum. I sent her some photos of the knife and what was left of the painted insignia, as well as the information regarding the blue pentacles on the sidewalk and the large red pentacle in the basement. She very kindly gave me her interpretation:

Now, the difference between a pentacle and a pentagram is this: A pentagram is simply a five-pointed star. It can be oriented up or down, if down it's satanic/demonic, if up it's a symbol of prosperity.

A Pentacle is a five-pointed star within a circle and all 5 points touch the circle's edge. Again, upright it's a symbol of prosperity, good health, and protection. It is rumored this is the sign that God gave to Solomon to grant him control over demons to have them build Solomon's temple in Jerusalem. Solomon himself was a High Magician. Pointed downward, it's a symbol to invite in dark forces.

A red pentacle or pentagram—not good. That's "red" magic. Red magic is used to control and manipulate the behavior, thoughts, and actions of others. You can use it in a benevolent manner to cleanse a person or location of evil spirits, but that's as far as I'd ever be willing to go with it as most of it beyond that is fairly dark stuff.

Blue pentacles or pentagrams—now this I have not heard of before, to be honest. Blue is associated with the water element, but the pentacle and pentagram both are of the earth element. So I am not sure what they were signifying with the blue pentacles/pentagrams. Blue is also healing. So it may be that the pentagram called in the stability and grounding of the earth element while the blue color made that pentacle be used for healing rituals/spell working.

The knife is an athame, a magical knife. Athames are not used for actually cutting items. They are used for raising and directing energy. The knife acts as an extension of the witch's arm and is a conduit for universal energies. To raise energy, the witch raises the athame above his/her head and then says whatever they would say in order to invoke the energy and channel it into the athame. In order to direct the energy, the athame is then pointed, usually at the altar or if the witch is charging some herbs, oils, or candles, the athame is pointed at those items. The energy then moves out and enters the item, thus giving it a magical charge for whatever purpose the witch intended. The skull and crossbones is a nice touch on this athame. Although most see that as a symbol of death or of pirates, the skull and crossbones can also serve as a warning to others to not mess with the item. Skull and crossbones can also be protective as well.

Items like this back then were probably more difficult to come by than today, I would imagine. I began practicing Wicca in 1980 and there was only ONE book I had as a reference and it was pretty impossible for me to find magical looking items for my altar.

To bury an athame, that is done for several reasons, first keep in mind this is a VITAL magical tool that is treated with the utmost respect because it conducts energy.

Reasons to bury an athame:

1. You bought a new one and want to retire the old one so you bury it out of respect.
2. For some reason, the athame becomes tainted and no longer conducts energy as well as it once did, so again, you would bury it out of respect.
3. Buried to serve as a protective ward. I am 95% positive the third reason is the thinking behind where the athame was positioned. As that is the only window well to the basement, it is the only point of entry from the outside. They were clearly conducting rituals in the basement. They would need that area to be magically sealed from all outside energies that may seek to interfere with the magical proceedings. That athame was most likely charged with protective and warding energy (a ward works to basically turn bad energy directed at you or a location away and sends it back to the sender), then buried in the window well to seal that window as a possible entryway.

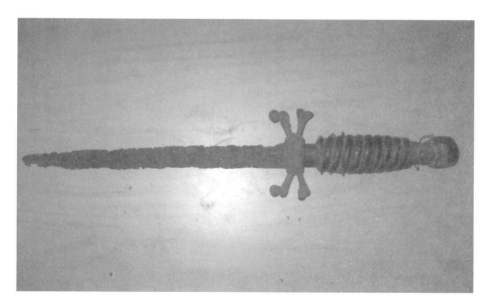

Ritual knife, or athame, bearing a skull and crossbones found buried in the window well of the basement of the Tonic Room.

Frederic De'Arechaga was not born with this name. He was actually born Manuel Nazario Rodriguez on July 28, 1935, in Havana, Cuba. He was admitted to the United States as a resident on April 14, 1954, and after a time in the U.S. Military, from 1954 to 1959, was granted U.S. citizenship on June 18, 1968. Pursuant to his petition for U.S. citizenship, he also petitioned that his name be legally changed to Frederic Manuel De'Arechaga with De'Arechaga being his mother's maiden name. That would make sense, since he claimed to be a "hereditary witch" from his mother's side of the family.

Before De'Arechaga was involved in the "El-Sabarum," he was also an accomplished artist. In the spring of 1961, he had designed a café in musician Ahmad Jamal's "Alhambra" at 1321 S. Michigan Avenue. De'Arechaga had claimed to have studied the original Alhambra firsthand in Granada, Spain, and the entrance of his café was modeled after the Court of Gold in the original Alhambra and the main room was modeled after The Court of Lions. He had painstakingly carved decorations out of Styrofoam and believed they were the only decorations of their kind. Unfortunately, within two years, the Alhambra closed its doors, only to reopen as The Taj Mahal with the new host being Col. S.M. Abdullah. While the place still looked like the Alhambra, and the music was still provided by the Ahmad Jamal trio, it was named after a place that was 10,000 miles away from the Alhambra, which probably did not sit well with the artist.

Sometime after 1974, De'Arechaga left the Sabaean Order and the Chicago area and ended up on Polymnia Street in New Orleans, Louisiana. He had changed his name to Odun after he converted to Santeria and started worshiping the god Obatala. Strangely enough, this seems quite fitting for an establishment named "The Tonic Room," since, according to Yoruban mythical lore, Obatala was the actual creator of human beings, and human beings were created with flaws because Obatala was drunk on palm wine when he created us!

According to a former student, Odun had suffered a stroke in 2005, retired as a teacher of "The Old Religion," and passed away quietly in his sleep on January 13, 2011.

Haunted History of a High School Landmark

I absolutely had to include this particular tale because it hits very close to home. I am speaking about the historic Chodl Auditorium that has been a part of J. Sterling Morton East High School in Cicero, Illinois since 1928. Cicero is Chicago's nearest west suburb and actually gave up some of its territory to be annexed to the City of Chicago to help increase Chicago's population during its successful bid for the Columbian Exposition of 1893. Of course, Cicero and Chicago will be forever linked to the infamous Al Capone who moved his base of operations to Cicero when things got a little too hot on the South Side of Chicago. The reason it hits so close to home for me is that Cicero was my hometown from 1971 until I was married in 1986.

When I was attending Morton East High School from 1980 to 1984, I had talked to a number of the older folks in town for a high school project and you could not say a bad word about Al Capone. He financed many of the soup kitchens in the town, as well as donating a good amount of money to local churches. Rumor had it when we were growing up that you couldn't find a Catholic Church in Cicero that didn't have some part of it donated by Al Capone. Of course, I don't know how true that was, but it made for great conversation!

The Chodl Auditorium was named after Edward W. Chodl, who was the president of the Board of Education from 1948 until his retirement in April 1975. Prior to that, it was simply known as the J. Sterling Morton High School Auditorium, but it was anything but simple. As a student, you don't always appreciate the finer things about your school because unless you were there when the school was erected, you just more or less took them for granted. I was guilty of that when I would sit in the Chodl Auditorium. Since I wasn't involved in the theater program, about the only time I was in the theater was during school-wide assemblies or meetings, which in my memory were usually pretty boring. Actually, it was probably a good thing that they were boring because I would start looking at the very cool murals on the upper walls of the theater and admire the high ceilings and the size of the stage. Even so, I really didn't appreciate what a great theater she was.

The original high school had its start as a three-story little red school house that was on Ogden and 59th Avenues. It was actually a combined grammar school and high school. On the first floor were two classrooms. On the second floor was an assembly, and on the third floor was a physics laboratory with a real skeleton in the closet! The first freshman class had a total enrollment of four girls and three boys. In 1897, the grammar school moved out and left the building entirely to the high school. In 1899, Mr. Harry Victor Church became the first principal of the Clyde Township High School, as it was known at the time.

As the community grew larger, it became necessary that the high school grow as well and the new school was erected in 1903 in its current location at 25th Street and Austin Avenue. It was named J. Sterling Morton High School in honor of Julius Sterling Morton, the originator of Arbor Day, Governor of Nebraska in 1888 and Secretary of Agriculture under President Cleveland in 1893. His son, Joy Morton, started the Morton Salt Company in 1848 in Chicago and also the Morton Arboretum in 1922. J. Sterling Morton died on April 27, 1902, the year before the new Morton High School was completed. There were several additions to the high school over the years and a fire on December 29, 1924, which destroyed the original sections of the high school but where replacement buildings were very quickly added.

The original combined Clyde Township grammar school and high school at the corner of 59th and Odgen Avenues. *Photograph courtesy of the Morton Archives, Cicero, IL.*

Henry Victor Church, first Principal of Morton High School was instrumental in procuring the Morton High School (Chodl) Auditorium. *Photograph courtesy of the Morton Archives, Cicero, IL.*

The school had a very robust music program, as well as a very successful athletics program that were spurred on by a large Czech population in Cicero and Berwyn that believed in physical fitness and theatrical performances. That combination and a very motivated Board of Education is what bolstered the successful completion of the new Auditorium. The Auditorium was completed in late 1927 at a cost of over $1 million, but its first performance was in January of 1928 and was a musical show. The combined orchestras of Morton, making a large assembly of approximately 180 pieces, opened the auditorium with "Largo" by Handel, and "Pizzacato" from "Ballet Sylvia" by Delibes. The boys and girls glee clubs were also involved and sang "Prayer of Thanksgiving," a Netherland folk song, and "The Glory of the Lord," by Handel. "Larghetto," by Mozart, was played by the violin choir as well. In a *Suburban Leader* newspaper article of January 12, 1928, Harry Church was quoted as saying:

> I have visited many schools all over the country and have not seen one auditorium more beautiful or larger than ours. It is a gift we may all be proud of, and has been completed at this time because of the untiring efforts of Mr. Tucker, the president of the Board of Education.

Mr. Church was not exaggerating. At the time, the now Chodl Auditorium was the largest non-commercial theater of its kind in the country and had the largest stage as well. The stage was large enough to hold a full court game of basketball and actually did for a great many years. It could seat over 2,500 audience members and had eight hand-painted oil on canvas murals by C.M. Fox of Marshall Field's Art Design Studio depicting historical events such as The Pilgrim's Landing, Lincoln's Giving the Gettysburg Address, Fort Dearborn, The Battle of Gettysburg, and The Battle of Argonne.

THE BELOVED DRAMA TEACHER WHO IS
"STAYING WAY AFTER SCHOOL"

I had only heard rumors of the theater being "haunted" when I was in school there and most of those probably came from my friends in the theater, but when I had gone on a nostalgic tour of my alma mater, I inquired about the haunting from the tour guide who had graduated

The first Morton High School building in 1903 at 25th and Austin Avenue.
Photograph courtesy of the Morton Archives, Cicero, IL.

The first addition to the original Morton High School.
Photograph courtesy of the Morton Archives, Cicero, IL.

Additions to the buildings were constructed surrounding the original buildings of the school.
Photograph courtesy of the Morton Archives, Cicero, IL.

Photograph of Thomas Newell from the 1928 "Mortonian" Yearbook. *Photograph courtesy of the Morton Archives, Cicero, IL.*

A 1928 sketch of the newly constructed auditorium by student and staff artist for the "Mortonian" yearbook, Thomas Newell. *Photograph courtesy of the Morton Archives, Cicero, IL.*

a few years before I started there. She replied without hesitation, "Oh, that would be Mr. Drew." She suggested that I contact Thomas Rusnak who knew Mr. Drew personally. One of the other tour goers was a friend of Mr. Rusnak and put me in touch. I knew the name was familiar and sure enough, he was the theater arts teacher when I was in high school.

We set up a meeting for breakfast at a small restaurant in Brookfield, Illinois, close to where we both live now. I didn't remember him by sight (again I wasn't in the theater program), but I did remember the name. The meeting went wonderfully and we shared names of some of my high school friends who were in the theater program, and what amazed me was that he had kept in touch with quite a few of them. I asked him about Mr.

Two views of oil and canvas murals painted by C.M. Fox of the Marshall Field Art Studios after the 1976 restoration of the auditorium. *Photographs courtesy of the Morton Archives, Cicero, IL.*

Drew and he smiled. He said that he liked to refer to the whole thing as the curse of *West Side Story*. He said that the school performed *West Side Story* in November of 1963, when President Kennedy was assassinated and the next time they performed it is when Mr. Drew died.

George John Drew was originally hired to be an art teacher in September 1966, after teaching at Riverside/Brookfield High School for six years, and was transferred over to the theater department. Tom remembered him loving his job and his students and the students loving him back.

It was November 12, 1976, opening night for *West Side Story* and Mr. Drew and the cast had just finished the dress rehearsal. They had put a huge amount of work into the play and Mr. Drew had asked a couple of the teachers if they would go out for an after-work drink with him, but nobody was able to, so he just went home to get ready for the evening. Tragically, he suffered a fatal heart attack before he could leave for the performance. It came as a huge blow to the students. Superintendent, Dr. Joseph Ondrus made the announcement of Mr. Drew's passing before the opening curtain and Frank Salamone, who was playing Bernardo, announced that the play was being dedicated to Mr. Drew. Mr. Drew had said earlier, "The cast and crew of *West Side Story* are very dedicated and enthusiastic and we are promising a spectacular performance which everyone will enjoy."

The students put aside their grief for the sake of the show and delivered a spectacular performance despite their loss. Mr. Drew's funeral was a traditional Greek funeral held at SS. Constantine and Helen Greek Orthodox Church in Chicago with his students acting as pallbearers. He was laid to rest at Evergreen Cemetery.

Tom Rusnak said that for some time after that the kids would claim they would hear things or that the curtains would move for no apparent reason. One time he mentioned that some students were using a Ouija board and he heard one of the girls scream, but he pretty much attributed that to kid's stuff and overactive imaginations—until he had an experience that still gives him goose bumps to this day.

It was in the early to mid 1980s when the theater class was working on a production and had broke for dinner. Tom said that he assumed everyone, including himself, had left the theater and would return after dinner, but when he returned, he was met by two students who had not gone to dinner, but had just hung out in the theater while everyone was gone. He didn't think it was a big deal that they stayed behind and it wasn't as though he wouldn't allow students to hang out there, since while they were in the theater program, the theater belonged to all of them. It was the bewildered looks on their faces that concerned him.

As he remembered, the students' names were Bill and Keith. They both came straight to him and told him about a strange person who was hanging around the theater after everyone had left. They said that they were sitting on the desk on the stage when they saw an older man who they didn't recognize walk across the stage. They called out to him to ask him if he needed help with anything, but the man just seemed to ignore them, walked to the edge of the stage, and looked out into the empty audience seats for a few seconds. He then turned and started walking toward the back of the stage. Both boys thought this was really weird and decided they

Mr. George Drew discusses the upcoming production with a student in one of the last photos taken of him. *Photograph courtesy of the Morton Archives, Cicero, IL.*

were going to corner the guy and find out who he was and why he was there. They watched him walk behind one of the curtains and Bill went one way while Keith went the other. All they saw was each other! The man had literally disappeared with no exits possible. Tom told me that both boys were very athletic and could have easily caught anybody who would have walked behind a curtain so close to where they were sitting.

He asked the boys to describe the man and he will never forget what they had told him. The boys said that the man was middle-aged, not very tall, with a slight belly. They said that he was wearing a three-button shirt, a checkered sport coat, and hush puppies on his feet. They described his features as balding with a comb-over style haircut, a larger nose, and a mustache. They also mimicked the manner in which he walked. Tom said that his hair literally stood on end because they had perfectly described Mr. Drew from the way he looked to the way he dressed, and even a very distinct type of walk that he had! These students had never worked with Mr. Drew because it was about ten years after he'd had the fatal heart attack, and even if they'd managed to have seen him in an old yearbook, there is no way that they would be able to mimic his walk!

**The Chodl Auditorium stage today with set
from** *Lend Me A Tenor*.

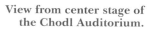

Two backstage views of the landmark Chodl
Auditorium where the spirit of Mr. Drew was
purportedly seen by two former drama students.

He didn't tell the boys anything about the fact that they had just described a deceased theater teacher and they went back to business as usual. Tom had never forgotten that encounter that the boys had and it never really scared him to be in the theater after that because, like he had said, Mr. Drew loved the theater and loved the kids.

Tom never heard of anyone else actually seeing Mr. Drew after that, but a good number of people have said that when they were in the theater alone, they did have a feeling as though someone was in the theater with them and others have seen curtains move or heard footsteps.

In March of 1983, after a seven-year process spearheaded by long-time drama teacher Jack Leckl, the Chodl was added to the National Register of Historic Places. Leckl was quoted in a *Chicago Tribune* article on March 30, 1983, calling the auditorium, "a monument to the immigrants who settled the Berwyn and Cicero area and their interest in fine arts."

I graduated from JSM with my future wife in 1984.

Edward W. Chodl, president of the Morton High School District Board of Education, from 1948 to 1975, speaks at his recognition celebration while Dr. J. Ondrus looks on. *Photograph courtesy of the Morton Archives, Cicero, IL.*

Exterior view of the Chodl Auditorium today.

Conclusion

Chicago has a wonderfully colorful and sometimes wonderfully strange history: there is seemingly no end to the number of amazing stories that are continually dug up by students, teachers, researchers—professional and amateur historians alike. The stories included in this book are only a very small fraction of the as-yet untold history of Chicago and its historical residents. I challenge all of those students out there who are bored with classical history to dig around some aged, dusty archives sometime, leaf through old books, manuscripts, microfilm, and file cabinets. You never know what secrets have been lying around waiting for someone like you to discover!

Bibliography and Suggested Readings

Bancroft, Hubert H. *The Book of the Fair: An Historical and Descriptive Presentation of the World's Science, Art, and Industry, As Viewed Through the Columbian Exposition at Chicago in 1893, Designed to Set Forth the Display Made by the Congress of Nations, of Human Achievement in Material Form, so As the More Effectually to Illustrate the Progress of Mankind in All the Departments of Civilized Life*. Chicago: The Bancroft Company, 1893. Print.

Bolotin, Norm, and Christine Laing. *The World's Columbian Exposition: The Chicago World's Fair of 1893*. Urbana: University of Illinois Press, 2002. Print.

Deuchler, Douglas. *Cicero Revisited*. Charleston, SC: Arcadia Pub, 2006. Print.

Fritscher, Jack. *Popular Witchcraft: Straight from the Witch's Mouth*. Bowling Green, Ohio: Bowling Green University Popular Press, 1972. Print.

Grossman, James R., Ann D. Keating, and Janice L. Reiff. *The Encyclopedia of Chicago*. Chicago: University of Chicago Press, 2004. Print.

Kay, Betty C. *Cicero: The First Suburb West*. Charleston, SC: Arcadia Pub, 2000. Print.

Larson, Erik. *The Devil in the White City: Murder, Magic, and Madness at the Fair That Changed America*. New York: Crown Publishers, 2003. Print.

Mudgett, Jeff. *Bloodstains: [based on a True Story]*. United States: s.n., 2011. Print.

Randall, Frank A. *History of the Development of Building Construction in Chicago*. Urbana: University of Illinois Press, 1949. Print.

Shaffer, Tamara. *Murder Gone Cold: The Mystery of the Grimes Sisters*. Oak Lawn, Il: Ghost Research Society Press, 2006. Print.

Index

4D Restaurant, 117
58th Illinois Regiment, 24
A.B.C. Copier Co., 58, 59, 60
Abdullah, Col. S.M., 140
Addams, Jane, 87, 96
Addergoole 14, 93, 94, 95
Adriatic, 80
Advertiser, 91
Alhambra, 140
Allen, H.W., 42
Ames, Julia, 88
Andersen, Judith Mae, 111, 113
Anderson, Chief Nels, 118
Andrews, Mrs. Thomas, 75, 77
Appleton Pulp and Paper Mill, 57
Art Institute of Chicago, 58, 68, 91
automatic writing, 88, 89

Bacon, Henry, 93
Battle of Gettysburg, 36, 144
Bedwell, Edward "Bennie", 115, 125
Belfast Morning News, 79
Benzkofer, Stephan, 126
Beveridge, Bruce, 5, 75, 115
Blenhuber, Robert, 42
Blomberg, Sharon, 125
Boston Courier, 91
Bourke, Catherine, 94
Bourke, John, 94, 95, 96
Bourke, Mary, 94, 96
Bradley, T.M., 24, 25
Breen, Phillip J., 40, 42
Brewster Apartments, 65, 67, 68, 72
Brighton Theater, 114, 125, 126
Britannic, 79

Bryan, Thomas Barbour, 12, 57, 58, 59, 60

Bryant, Marian, 100

Burke, Father, 21

Burnham, Daniel H., 32, 38, 40, 61, 62, 92

Butt, Major Archibald Willingham, 92, 93

Cahill, John, 40, 42

Calvary Cemetery, 25, 41, 42

Campbell, Hiram S., 60

Canadian Grand Trunk Railroad, 79

Canavan, Mary, 94

Canavan, Patrick, 94, 95, 96

Capone, Al, 141, 142

Carlson, Hugo, 84

Carpathia, 83, 96, 97, 98

Catholic Women's League, 97

Ceduldid, Henry, 42

Chicago Courthouse, 9, 10, 11

Chicago Fire Department, 31, 32, 40-43, 45

Chicago History Museum, 67

Chicago Intermediate Company, 59

Chicago Police Department, 114, 128

Chicago River, 56, 64,

Chicago's Haunt Detective, 7, 112

Child's Play, 65

Chodl Auditorium, 141-144, 150-152

Chodl, Edward W., 142, 152

Church of St. Columbkille, 21

Church, Harry Victor, 142-144

Cigrand, Emaline C., 64

Civil War, 7, 36, 91, 92

Clark, Florence, 100

Clyde Township High School, 142, 143

Colburn, John, 14

Cold Storage Building, 31, 32, 34, 35, 37-39, 42, 43, 45

Collins, Pheobe, 10

Collins, William H., 70, 72

Colton, Walter R., 12, 13

Columbus, Christopher, 30, 37, 39, 43, 45

Connor, J.L., 49

Connor, Julia, 49, 50, 57, 60, 62

Connor, Pearl, 62

Connors, Jack, 5, 45

Cook County Sheriff's Office, 47, 57, 60, 100, 115, 118, 119, 122, 129

Cook, Barry, 125

Corbett, William, 17 - 26

Corbus, Dr. Budd Clarke Jr., 84

Cottage Grove, 22, 37, 40

Cottage Hill, 10, 12, 58

Cox, Albert E., 102

Crowe, Richard, 106

Custer Park, 52

D&L Restaurant, 115

Daib, Frederick, 70

Daib, Frieda, 70

De'Arechaga, Frederic, 132-134, 140

Denning, William H., 41

Deveaney, Sgt. William, 118

Devil's Creek, 114

Donohoe, Bridget, 94

Dredling, John, 84

Drew, George John, 146, 148, 149, 151, 152

Drummond, Ralph H., 40

Durkee, Kate, 58-61

Durkee, Mary, 58

Edwards, Bjoerne, 67-70, 72

Edwards, Mary C.C., 70

Elgin State Mental Hospital, 116, 117

Elmhurst, 9, 10, 12, 14, 58, 97, 118

Elmhurst Historical Museum, 13, 15

Elmhurst Library, 14

Elmhurst Park District, 14

El-Sabarum, 132-134, 137

Engine Co. 123, 43

Engine Co. 51, 43

England, Liverpool, 52, 53, 89

Englewood, 37, 47, 49, 52

Evergreen Cemetery, 148

execution, 21-24, 26, 27, 30

Ferlic, Frank, 119

Ferris, George, 30

Finan, James, 18, 20, 24

Fire Museum of Greater Chicago, 5, 34, 35, 43, 45

First Folio Theater, 110

Fisher, Gustave, 24, 25

Fitzpatrick, Captain James, 33, 36, 40

Flaherty, Ellen, 94

Fleming, Nora, 94

Fleming, Patrick, 17-26

Flynn, James, 94

Folz, C., 24

Ford Center for the Performing Arts, 83

Fox, C.M., 144, 147

Franciscan Province of the Sacred Heart, Order of Friars Minor, 102

Frank, Louis J., 41

Franklin, Philip, 81

Freeman, Lt. John H., 41

Freer, Dr. J.W., 25

French, Daniel Chester, 93

Fritscher, Dr. Jack, 132, 133, 154

Futility, 77

Garden City Banking and Trust Company, 60

Garvey, Cpt. James A., 40, 42

Gary, Judge, 20

German Church Road, 111, 114

Gigantic, 79

Gilbert, James H., 60, 61

Graceland Cemetery, 56, 58, 93

Gracie, Colonel Archibald, 79

Green, Emma Wadhams, 13, 14

Green, Francis W., 51, 52

Green, William, 47, 49-57, 59-64

Greene, Mary, 94, 98

Grimes, Barbara, 111, 114-116, 122, 126

Grimes, Dr. P.D., 118

Grimes, Loretta, 114, 125, 129

Grimes, Patricia, 111, 114-116, 122, 123, 126

Grimes, Theresa, 128

Gubbins, Willliam, 18-20

Harland and Wolff, 79-81

Harrison, William, 30

Hartman, Norman M., 37, 42

Hartz, Henry L., 61

Harvard University, 57, 91

Hayes-Richards Circle, 93

Haymarket Riot, 109

Hays, Charles, 79

Hearst, William Randolph, 54

Hearthstone, 56

Hearthstone Historic House Museum, 56

Henney, Charles, 24

Henry J. Rogers & Co., 62

Hercules Iron Works Company, 31, 37, 38

Herrebout, Kathleen, 5, 94

Hippach, Archibald A., 82

Hippach, Gertrude (Jean) B., 82, 83, 85, 86

Hippach, Howard H., 82, 83, 84

Hippach, Ida, 82, 83, 84

Hippach, Louis A., 82, 83, 84

Hippach, Robert L., 82

Hletko, Dr. Paul, 122, 123

Holland, Frederick Eugene, 10

Holmes, H.H., 47-52, 54-62

Holy Cross Cemetery, 64

Holy Name Cathedral, 97

Home Safety Deposit Vault Company, 53

Horan, Chief Fire Marshal James, 31

Howorth, Chrissie, 5, 110

Hitchins, Doris, 116, 118

If Christ Came to Chicago, 87

Illinois Bank Building, 59

Illinois, Cicero, 118, 141, 143, 145-147, 149, 152, 154

Illinois, Lake Forest, 84

Iroquois Theater, 82, 83

Ismay, Bruce, 80

J. Sterling Morton East High School, 5, 141, 142

Jackson Park, 30, 31, 43, 93
Jackson, William, 22
Jacobs, H.E., 57
Jamal, Ahmad, 140
Jenney, W.L.B., 68
Joseph, Sister Patrick, 97, 98
Jub Jub Club, 134
Julia's Bureau, 88
Kelly, Anna Katherine, 93, 94
Kelly, John, 94, 95, 97
Kelly, Mary, 5, 58, 59, 98
Kendelin, Peter, 19
Kennedy, John, 18-20, 24, 26, 27
Kenyon, Chief Joseph, 43
Khepri, Dr. Nefer, 5, 137
Kimberly-Clark's Vulcan Mill, 57
Kleen, Michael, 131
Koz, Rich, 131
Kranz, Walter, 124
Kuta, Stanley, 77
Lang, James, 131
Langley, Deputy Sheriff Edward, 16, 21
Larson, Erik, 47, 154
Lathrop, Jedediah, 12
Leckl, Jack, 152
Lincoln Park Palace, 67, 68, 70
Linton, George, 84
Lord Pirrie, 81
Loring, Edward R., 12
Love Me Tender, 114, 125
Lovering, Clara, 61
MacKay Bennett, 92
Mahon, Bridget, 94
Mahoney, W.P., 36
Majestic, 53, 89
Maloney, Hanora, 18
Maloney, James, 19
Maloney, Patrick, 17-19
Mangan, Mary, 94
Manufacturers and Liberal Arts Building, 30
Marshall Field's Art Design Studio, 144

Marshall, Benjamin, 102
Mather, Robert, 54
Mayflower, 91
Mayslake Farm, 5, 100-102, 104-106, 108
McAvoy Brewing Company, 100
McAvoy, John H., 100
McBride, John C., 41
McDermott, Bridget Delia, 93-96
McDermott, Michael, 19
McDonnell, Robert, 119
McGowan, Anna, 93, 94, 96
McGowan, Katherine, 94
McKinley Park, 125, 129
McMenamin, Frank, 5, 45
McMullen, Rev., Dr., 21, 25
McNalis, Father John, 5, 45
McNamee, Jane, 22
McNamee, Michael, 22, 23
McQuade, M., 42
Melody, Delia, 95
Melquist, Charles, 117-124, 129
Melquist, Elmer, 117
Merchant's Loan and Trust Company, 100
Merrill, Deputy Sheriff, 16, 21
Metropolitan Banking and Trust Company, 60
Millet, Francis D., 91-93
Mock, Phillip, 90
Monon Building, 59
Montrose Harbor, 111, 113
Morton Arboretum, 142
Morton Salt Company, 142
Morton, Joy, 142
Morton, Julius Sterling, 142
Mount St. Mary's College, 51, 52
Moyamensing Prison, 54, 56
Mudgett, Herman Webster, 47, 48
Murphy, Bernard, 42
Murphy, Captain Edward A., 31
Murphy, Father, 21, 24

Nillson, Helmina Josefina, 77

Nind, Frederick George, 58-60

North American, 72

Northwestern Dental School, 83

O'Connor, Rev., Father, 35, 36

O'Herigan, Henry, 54

O'Malley, Dr. Thomas J., 97

Oakwoods Cemetery, 29, 39, 40-42

Oakwoods Memorial Chapel, 43

Obatala, 140

Old People's Home of Chicago, 13, 14

Ondrus, Dr. Joseph, 148, 152

Our Lady of Good Counsel, 97

Page, Cpt. Burton E., 42

Pall Mall Gazette, 87

Peabody & Co.

Peabody Energy, 106

Peabody, Daniels & Co., 100

Peabody, Francis B., 100

Peabody, Francis Stuyvesant, 100, 102, 106, 108, 110

Peabody, Harriet, 100

Peabody, May, 100, 101

Peabody, Stuyvesant, 100, 101

Pease, Harry, 24

Peterson, Robert, 111

Phelps, Robert E., 64

Philadelphia Centennial Exposition, 91

Philadelphia Inquirer, 54

Phillip Brennan's Saloon, 18, 19

Pierson, John, 17

Pitezel, Benjamin, 56, 60, 64

Plummer, Wharton, 59-61

Porter, Dr. Mary O'Brien, 97

Portiuncula Chapel, 102, 106

Prescott, Leonard, 114

Presley, Elvis, 114

Prunty, Diane, 125

Purvis, Lt. Charles W., 41

R.M.S. *Lusitania*, 89

R.M.S. *Titanic*, 29, 75-81, 83-87, 89, 90, 92, 94-97

Raymond-Greiner, Mary, 72

Rea, Dr. R.L., 25

Rehfeldt, Hans, 36

Reid Institute, 119

Reid, John E., 118

Resurrection Larry, 131

Resurrection Mary, 75, 131

Resurrectionist, 25

Review of Reviews, 87

Rice, John Blake, 17

Riddell, Gerard J., 51-54, 57

Riddle, Gerard J., 51

Robertson, Morgan, 77, 78

Roche, Captain John, 119

Rodriguez, Manuel Nazario, 140

Rogers, Cremora, 56

Rogers, Florence, 56

Rogers, Henry J., 49, 55, 57, 60, 62

Rookery Building, 61, 62

Roosevelt, Theodore, 92

Root, John, 61, 62

Rosehill Cemetery, 40, 72, 82, 87

Rowland, John, 77

Royal Academy of Fine Arts, 91

Rusnak, Thomas, 5, 146, 148

Sabaean Religious Order, 132, 140

Saint-Gaudens, Augustus, 91

Salamone, Frank, 148

Sand Ridge, 17, 19

Santa Fe Park, 124

Schroeder, Paul W., 42

Schuba, Chris, 134

Schuba, Michael, 134

Schuessler, Anton Jr., 111

Schuessler, John, 111

Schwolow, Marilyn, 116

Schwolow, Robert H., 116

Scott, Bonnie Leigh, 116-125, 129

Scott, J.W., 58

Sears, Richard Warren, 82

Shedd, John G., 82

Shields, Beth, 5, 14, 27

Shipbuilder, 80

Sisters of Charity, 21

Six Mile House, 17, 18

Smith, Captain E. J., 80, 81, 89

Smith, Hazel, 117

Smith, John A., 42

Spencer, Earl, 90

Spirit of the Jail, 16

SS. Constantine and Helen Greek Orthodox Church, 148

St. Mary's University, 21

St. Phillip Neri, 97

St. Rita, 97

St. Vincent Hospital, 96

Staub, Albert, 22

Stead, William T., 87-90

Stone, John, 22

Straube, Anna F., 98

Strong, General Henry, 70

Svengoolie, 131

Temple of the Moon, 132-134

Tenney, Church & Coffeen, 60

Teutonic, 52

The Devil in The White City, 47, 62

The Exorcist, 133

The Most Honourable Order of the Bath, 90

The Taj Mahal, 140

Thomas Kelly High School, 114, 126, 127

Thomson, Lucretia, 22

Tillman, Kirsten, 5, 14, 27

Titanic: The Ship Magnificent, 77

Tonic Room, 5, 131-137, 139, 140

Toring, Malek A., 38

Trinity Church, 91

Turner, Major General Sir Alfred Edward, 90

Turnock, Enoch Hill, 68

Twentieth Century Limited, 83, 84

Tyler and Hippach Co., 82, 84

Unander-Scharin, Consul Egil, 84

Unander-Scharin, Kahalmar, 84-86

Union Signal of Chicago, 88

University of Michigan, 48

Vanaria, Denise, 5, 75

Wadhams, Dana, 10, 12

Wadhams, David, 10

Wadhams, Elizabeth, 13, 15

Wadhams, Emma, 10, 12, 13

Wadhams, Seth, 9, 10, 12-16, 27

Wadhams, Willard & Co., 10

Waits, Tom, 5, 134

Waters, William, 56

Wayman, William, 24

Wentworth, Mayor John "Long John", 82

West Side Story, 148

Western Edison Light Company, 57

White Birch, 10, 13, 27

White Star Line, 52, 80, 81, 89, 94

Wiedrich, Robert, 122

Wilder Park, 9, 10, 12, 14

Wilder, Thomas, 9, 10, 14

William A. Bond & Co., 51

William Green & Co., 49, 50, 56, 57, 59, 60, 62, 64

Williams, John, 17-19

Willow Springs Police Department, 114

Willowbrook High School, 117

Wisconsin, Appleton, 50, 56, 57

Women's Christian Temperance Movement, 88

World's Columbian Commission

World's Columbian Exposition, 29, 31, 34, 43, 47, 56-58, 75, 80, 87, 91, 92, 141, 154

Yeadon, Pennsylvania, 64

York High School, 116

Zatas, Edward, 118

Zelko, Mollie, 118